Reclaiming the Ivory Tower

Reclaiming the Ivory Tower
Organizing Adjuncts to Change Higher Education

Joe Berry

Monthly Review Press

Library of Congress Cataloging-in-Publication

Berry, Joe.
　Reclaiming the ivory tower: organizing adjuncts to change higher education / by Joe Berry.
　　p. cm.
　　ISBN 1-58367-129-3 (pbk.)-ISBN 1-58367-130-7 (cloth)

　　1. College teachers, Part-time--United States. 2. Universities and colleges—United States—Faculty. 3. College teachers' unions—United States. 4. Universities and colleges—Employees—Labor unions—Organizing—United States. I. Title.
　　LB1778.2.B47 2005
　　378.1'2--dc22

　　　　　　　　　　　　　　　　　　　　　　　　2005024451

MONTHLY REVIEW PRESS
122 West 27th Street
New York, NY 10001
www.monthlyreview.org

Printed in United States of America

10 9 8 7 6 5 4 3 2 1

To Helena Worthen, who always said I should and could do it, that she would help me, and did not lie. And to David Wakefield, fellow student, colleague, activist, and dear friend and comrade, who inspired so much in me and died so young.

Contents

Introduction

An old friend tells me about an old friend of his who just got a tenured position at a University of California campus. Pretty unremarkable occurrence, until you realize that this particular acquaintance has been a temporary, full-, and part-time college teacher for well over a decade. In that time he has published four books, a couple of them bestsellers in his field, and won a MacArthur "Genius" Award. This newly job-secure professor actually had to be a certified genius before he could get a permanent teaching job in a college in the second-largest metropolitan area of the United States, Southern California.

Another contingent teacher, this time in Chicago, had a phone conversation with a dean who might have a class open for the upcoming academic term. The dean has been bemoaning dropping enrollments at the college. The applicant asks sympathetically, "Have you had any layoffs?"

"No," replies the dean, "we've just cut adjuncts."

At a conference of contingent faculty from all over North America, after a few drinks, the talk turns to retirement. No one in the discussion is under thirty and most are well over forty. One New Yorker, after listening for a time, drops his one-liner: "My only retirement plan is a bullet in my dresser drawer."

A student and teacher in a post-class huddle over some problems the student is having. Clearly more time and privacy are needed for this talk. Suddenly, the teacher looks at her watch and tells the student that she must leave this instant to get to her other college miles ways where her class starts in an hour. She reminds the student of her regular office half hour and asks to continue the discussion then. As she turns to leave, the student fatalistically tells her that he can't come then because his boss will fire him if he leaves work early one more time. They look at each other speechlessly, then both turn and walk away, defeat emanating from their slumped shoulders.

In one of the largest community colleges in the United States, a small group of part-time faculty has nearly finished their conversation with the college vice president in his office. As they rise to leave, the VP pulls the leader, a longtime teacher with a Ph.D., aside and, in a low voice, tells him, "You know, I really support what you are trying to do for part-timers, but you should realize that you are not considered faculty, or even people. You are units of flexibility."

A letter arrives at many Chicago area college department offices offering a new commercial service: prescreening and referring adjuncts to college hiring officials. Investigation reveals that it is an attempt at a start-up company by an adjunct who cannot get a tenure track job himself.

A young single mother and part-time student at a community college comes back to register for classes after taking a semester or two off. She looks at the class schedule and sees nearly all the courses in her major are taught by either "staff" or "TBA." She asks in her department about a particular teacher whose classes she enjoyed previously, hoping to take another or at least get some advice from this teacher. She is told her teacher was a part-timer and is no longer at the school and may or may not ever return.

An artist who also teaches at two colleges is denied part of her unemployment insurance claim against one of the colleges because she has "reasonable assurance of re-employment" for the following term, which of course she does not have. Partially as a result, she can't pay her apartment rent and has to move, illegally, into her art studio.

After twenty-five years of teaching, often more than full-time, but at multiple institutions, a California community college part-timer discovers he never received enough "service credit" for vesting in the retirement pension system. Only his actual time in the classroom was counted as working hours, unlike full-time faculty, so he did not qualify.

Another contingent teacher has to choose between rent and food for her child or health insurance premiums. She chooses food. She is better off than her colleague who, with a preexisting condition, cannot buy health insurance at any price. The loss of just one class, for low enrollment or many other reasons, would mean a drop below subsistence.

At a major private university in Chicago, an adjunct receives an e-mail from the retired president of the university informing her that he will be teaching the class she has taught for years. He also asks if she could give him her syllabus, since she is the only one who has *ever* taught the course, and meet him for lunch ("any day except Thursday") to "chat about the course." The adjunct is grateful

List of Terms Used for Regular Faculty

Regular
Full-time
Tenured or tenure-track
Permanent
Senate
Ranked (as in not having academic rank)
Voting
Department member
Faculty
Professor: Full, Associate, Assistant
Core
Presidential appointment
Traditional

Standard
Salaried
Teacher-of-record
Hard money
Line (as in having a budget line)
Continuing
Continuing contract
Standing
Internal
Academic
Ladder
Contract

List of Terms Used for Contingent Faculty

Contingent
Part-time
Nontenure-track
Visiting (various ranks)
Temporary
Occasional
Non-Senate
Unranked (not having academic rank)
Adjunct
Instructor
Lecturer
Casual
Limited term
Dean's appointment
Student (graduate)
Peripheral
New model
Non-traditional
Non-standard
Hourly
Section leader
Sessional
Yearly
Soft money
Grant-funded

Non-line (not having a budget line)
Fixed term
External
Community-based
Clinical
Applied
Non-regular
Extension
Continuing Education
Non-academic
Non-remunerated
Non-ladder
Wives or faculty wives
Emergency wife
Emergency hire
Ad hoc
Assistant
Graduate assistant
Teaching assistant
Teaching associate
specialist
Nonvoting
Contract
Limited contract

From: Worthen, Helena, and Joe Berry. Contingent Faculty in Public Higher Education in Pennsylvania, Spring 1999: Focus on the Community Colleges. Harrisburg, PA: Keystone Research Center, 1999.

that it is still early enough not to waste one of her formal "course requests" to her supervisor for this class.

Welcome to the new world of higher education where, in any given semester, well over half of the nearly million teaching faculty in the United States are working as the academic equivalent of day labor. For those of you who have been outside the ivied walls for many years, this may come as a shock. Even for many inside the walls —students, tenured faculty, other staff—the amount of the transformation may still be surprising. However, for those of us doing most of the work of teaching in post-secondary and adult education, it is a depressingly familiar reality. This book is addressed to all those with an interest in the present reality and future potential of higher education. It is particularly addressed to my colleagues, the contingent majority faculty, the new majority faculty, who every day carry our multiple bulging briefcases, backpacks, and other carryalls into tens of thousands of classrooms—classrooms that are filled with students who have no idea that the "professor" standing before them, doing all the visible work that they expect, is likely working for less per hour than many of those paying tuition and working part-time somewhere else.

This book is not meant to be yet another library-filling volume bemoaning, describing, explaining, or justifying these changes in the academic workforce. If there is one thing academics can do to excess, besides talk, it is write. Therefore, I felt I needed a very good reason before I added my tree killings to the thousands of existing books and articles. And the reason is that there is not one book, and very few articles, that actually tell contingent faculty and their friends and allies how they might go about changing this situation. This is meant to be a book of ideas for change, a manual for action, with just enough background description of the general context to make the strategies and tactics understandable. Mostly, I will talk about what folks like us have done, what worked and what didn't, through the voices and stories of our colleagues who took a chance and became "troublemakers." I am indebted to Dan LaBotz for his use of the term in his justly famous *Troublemakers Handbook: How to Fight Back Where You Work and Win,* its 2005 edition edited by Jane Slaughter. The general idea for the framework and goals of this book owes a lot to Dan and his example.

In other words, I will share useful history from the thirty years and more of contingent faculty activism. Integrated with this history are lessons we can draw from that experience. They form a framework for how we might move forward and give a set of examples for what each of us might do. They also let us know that we are part of a huge campus labor force that has created a vibrant labor movement, including clerical and technical workers, grad employees, food service, maintenance, and housekeeping workers, university hospital workers, skilled trades people, and academic professionals of all sorts. This movement has spanned the entire spectrum of post-secondary education, from urban adult educators teaching ESL to contingent professors teaching graduate students at the most elite universities.

The collective knowledge of these decades of activity has seldom been put together in a form that is accessible, readable, and pointed in the direction of improving our situation. This book is my attempt to do that. The many phone calls and e-mails and letters I have received over my own twenty-plus years as a non-tenure track teacher and activist suggest to me that thousands of faculty out there are ready to act if only they (we) had some guidance and encouragement. Thousands more are already acting, and this book is for you, too. Since 1995 a national, and now international, movement has emerged to battle on behalf of us as professional workers in higher education. Sometimes generically referred to as COCAL—Conferences On Contingent Academic Labor—this book owes its existence to this movement. For those already in motion, and for those getting started, I hope to save you some mistakes. Learn from others' mistakes, and then go out and make more of your own. Then tell the rest of us what happened.

This book is also for our tenure-track colleagues who often express sympathy with us in private but often seem not to know how to help us with solidarity, not charity, in practice. Finally, this book is for students, their parents who often are paying the bills, grad employees looking toward "regular" faculty jobs, former students, former contingent faculty, and all those who care about where one of our major social institutions is headed.

If this book has a single message it is this: first, there is a movement out there to learn from and join, and secondly, when we fight we are winning. That message makes this a fundamentally happy book, despite many stories of suffering, abuse, arrogance, duplicity, exploitation, and downright evil that are part of our daily lives. This book is also optimistic because of the work itself, work that we do every day with some of the most wonderful, though often poorly served, people in the world, our students. The last thirty years have seen the transformation of college faculty into a casualized majority. These years have also seen the transformation of the college student body from an elite, overwhelmingly white, mostly male, middle- and upper-class group into a body that much more nearly reflects the working class majority of the United States. Many of these students are ill prepared, underfinanced, overworked, and heavily distracted by a million and one other adult responsibilities in an economy of shrinking opportunities. Teaching them challenges us every single day. And every day (or nearly every day) we are glad we found this work to do. Now together we must figure out how to turn what has always been *good work* into *good jobs* that can give us a decent living and the conditions that allow us to do our best work. When we have done that, we will have given something of great value back—to a higher education system, which may not always deserve our efforts, and to our students, who certainly do.

The lessons outlined here are important not only to the growing campus labor movement but to rebuilding the whole labor movement. Our coalition experiences with other campus workers and students, our example as a casualized majority who are self-unionizing anyway, our majority female membership, and our multiple-job careers make us prototypes for the new union members of the future. A resurgent labor movement needs us and the lessons and skills we can bring to it. We need the rest of the working-class movement to help make us "all that we can be"—as teachers, workers, and activists.

1

Contingent Faculty Today: Who We Are

If you have read this far, you know something is wrong in higher education as a place of work and learning. You also know that a few anecdotes will not convince anyone to risk trying to change things. That needs a more solid rationale.

Higher education in the United States, unlike much of the rest of the world, is now a wild mix of public (state-owned and supported) and privately owned, both nonprofit and for-profit. Most of the degree-granting schools are licensed by the various states to do business and accredited as to their programs by regional accrediting groups, recognized by the federal government. There are also a variety of private, mainly for-profit, proprietary career colleges, trade schools, and other specialized institutions. Many do not grant degrees but instead give certificates of completion in a particular course of study. These schools may be accredited by an institutional body within a particular field, such as career colleges or language schools. The whole regulatory and accrediting structure is currently in flux, especially under the challenges of distance education and the rise of for-profit specialized institutions.

Within traditional degree-granting higher education, the top group are major research universities, which generally grant Ph.D.'s and often include professional schools in law, medicine, education, etc., as well as undergraduate colleges. These are both public and private. Most have also developed large, and profitable, extension or evening programs to tap into the adult learner market, staffed mostly by contingent faculty. They depend upon contingents for most undergraduate instruction, mainly graduate employees. Private self-perpetuating boards of trustees govern the private universities while public boards, usually appointed by state governors, rule the public institutions.

Next there are four-year universities that focus upon teaching, not research, and generally do not grant doctoral degrees, but many have master's programs.

Some of these were formerly teachers colleges that expanded into universities. Most of these are public, but many are also private "comprehensive" universities, especially in large cities. Examples include Roosevelt University in Chicago and the California state university system. Most of these also employ many full- and part-time contingent teachers and some now use M.A. students as graduate teachers in large numbers.

Making up another group are the traditional private, nonprofit liberal arts colleges, often with religious origins, that focus upon bachelor degree programs. Under economic pressure many of these are adding specialized vocational undergraduate and graduate programs and satellite campuses in areas of greatest potential profit. Their shrinking numbers include elite, expensive schools such as Bennington, as well as local area colleges that dot the Midwest. This is perhaps the only group of colleges where contingents are not the majority, but this is changing as some colleges alter their mission and geography.

Two-year schools, mainly public and usually called community colleges, granting associate degrees and preparing students for transfer, are the single biggest part of traditional higher education. They also have many non-degree vocational certificate programs and offer large non-credit adult education programs in both basic skills and personal enrichment. Historically these schools were tuition-free and grew out of the public school systems after World War Two, but all now charge tuition, some substantial. They remain the most economical and accessible alternative for most students and for many occupations have taken over training that used to be found on the job and/or via apprenticeships. About two-thirds of all community college faculty are part-time temporary and have been since the 1980s.

The new entries into the degree-granting schools are the proprietary, for-profit institutions, such as DeVry and University of Phoenix, which are the fastest growing of all. They have branches all over the United States, Canada, and elsewhere, and focus upon high-demand fields of study. They also have developed graduate education in areas such as business. They particularly focus upon working adult students and stress convenience and quick time to a degree. They charge more than most public colleges, but less than most privates. Their faculty are nearly all part-time temporary. These schools are an addition on a major scale to degree-granting higher education, many having grown by merger and acquisition, as favorites with Wall Street. Most make extensive use of Web-based distance education, with a few being completely Web-based. Their accreditation has been controversial in some circles. Some estimate that the faculty of the for-profit sector may total as much as all of traditional higher education combined, meaning a million or more.

A final degree-granting sector is the specialized school, sometimes unaccredited. These include Bible or clerical training colleges, experimental or other schools too small for accreditation, specialized freestanding professional schools, such as in psychology, business, or law, limited residency programs, and a variety of outright scam diploma mills. This "nontraditional" sector is listed and explained in the famous *Bear's Guide to Earning College Degrees Nontraditionally*, by John and Mariah Bear. This sector has also exploded due to the increasing demand for degree credentials. There is almost no documentation on this faculty segment, but my personal contacts suggest that virtually none have full tenure and many are part-time.

Non-credit, non-degree higher education is even more varied. There are the traditional proprietary trade schools, some of which have moved into granting associate degrees as well. There are also large subdivisions of traditional universities doing non-credit instruction as continuing education, often quite profitably. There are thousands of specialized schools teaching adults everything from foreign languages (Berlitz et al.) to how to sew (classes in Singer sewing machine stores). There are also in-house training programs in many companies, some "corporate universities" with elaborate campuses and relations with traditional educational institutions. Many of the teachers in these programs are considered independent contractors and often work part-time as well. As public adult education programs connected to K-12 school districts or to community colleges have shrunk due to budget cuts, the private sector has moved in, at least in those areas where it seems a profit can be made. Basic adult education such as English as a Second Language (ESL) for working-class immigrants or high school equivalency (GED) programs have declined, though some nonprofit community groups and churches have tried to take up the slack, often hustling for grants to do so. This is the sector that is least documented, though it employs many thousand of instructors, many of whom also teach in degree-granting contexts.

Corporatization: Higher Education in the Service of Capital

Higher education, like much of the rest of American society, has become more market oriented and corporate in the last thirty years. I will discuss the impact this has on faculty and administrators in later sections, but the main point here is that this "corporatization" has arrived in two ways. Traditional institutions have internally mimicked their successful for-profit competitors by becoming more profit than service oriented. Also, higher education has been restructured externally to more directly serve the needs of private business, which is now considered the ultimate customer to whom students are provided as trained workers. Students themselves are now also seen as customers to be trained and wooed rather than as citizens to be educated, especially in tuition-dependent institutions.

All of private higher education—degree granting or not, for-profit or not—is heavily dependent on their students' getting federally subsidized tuition assistance, in the form of both loans and grants. The only exceptions are the few wealthiest institutions, which can operate off endowment income. Yet, even the elite universities are dependent on government research funds. Without these federal subsidies, most of U.S. private higher education would fold. In this sense, they are privately owned and controlled, but largely publicly financed. Public institutions have become more tuition dependent in recent years as direct state support has fallen. This has made them more "entrepreneurial" and also made them more dependent upon federal student aid, just like their private competitors. They have also become more dependent on private gifts to build endowments and private foundations, again imitating the privates.

The casualization of the faculty workforce is the leading edge of this corporatization. It represents one of the few recent instances in the United States economy (another is taxi driving) where an entire occupation has been converted from permanent career status to temporary, often part-time, status in the space of a single generation of workers. This casualized majority is less uniform than the old professoriate and includes part-timers hired class by class, full-time temporaries on contracts of varying length, and graduate employees. As a group, we are often called adjuncts, but since we are now the majority, that term seems less accurate. I will refer to the entire group as contingents, since what mainly separates us from our full-time tenured and tenure track (FTTT) colleagues is our permanent lack of permanence. While graduate employees are certainly contingent college teachers (and researchers), I am excluding them from most of my generalizations, unless noted otherwise. This is because their situation as both students and employees is different from the rest of us and also because they have built a primarily separate set of organizations and unions.

The idea and practice of "tenure" for academics has come under attack, both by higher education administrators and by powerful figures in the society at large. As a result, many in the public have come to question the "privilege" enjoyed by some academics. The idea of tenure is simply the right to possession of one's job after having been proved competent during a four- to six-year probation (called tenure track), unless the employer can show through due process a just cause for dismissal. Tenure does not protect from layoffs for economic reasons, but firing for cause. Tenured faculty *are* fired every year, but it is a cumbersome and demanding process for administrators and one they would like to avoid. This is similar in practice to the "just cause discipline and discharge" language found in most union contracts. However, historically the special case for academic tenure has been that the freedom to search for and speak the truth as one sees it (academic freedom) is not possible except under conditions of tenure-like job security. If one is afraid of being fired, one will, naturally, tend to watch one's tongue. Since it is not in the public interest to have students taught by people who are afraid to speak the truth as they see it, tenure has been seen as a public good.

Now that most teachers in higher education have neither tenure nor the prospect of ever getting it, administrators and trustees have won a great victory. They have much greater flexibility to hire and fire as program and enrollment demands, and the faculty as a whole is less able to set the terms of its own work. So, as tenured faculty retire, many of their jobs are converted into non-tenured contingent ones.

A Few Statistics

Driven by both the desire for flexibility and tightening economics, administrators have transformed the teaching force since the 1970s. The figures documenting this have mostly come from a compilation of various reports of the National Center for Educational Statistics of the U.S. Department of Education. There are problems with the figures, which are discussed in the note at the end of the chapter. In 1970, 68 percent of new Ph.D.'s found university or college full-time tenure-track positions. Post-1980, only 51 percent did, even though enrollment was up 41 percent between 1970 and 1980. The prospects have not improved since. Looked at a different way, from 1917 to 1986 the number of part-timers increased 133 percent while the number of full-timers increased only 22 percent. Sometime in the 1990s the majority of teachers became contingent, either part-time or full-time temporary. If graduate employees, employees of for-profits, and teachers of non-credit classes were counted here, the "contingent majority" date would be earlier and percentage much higher now.

Even among full-time faculty, the majority of new hires since 1995 have been off the tenure track (FTNTT), and now over 24 percent of full-time faculty at institutions with a tenure system have no hopes of tenure. A few places have even tried to abolish tenure for existing FTTT faculty, but this usually has been successfully resisted. However, tenure protections have often been weakened and requirements for getting tenure have been increased.

Within academic disciplines, a study focusing primarily upon arts, humanities, and social sciences departments found that the percentage of full-timers ranged from 50 to 65 percent. If we subtract the non–tenure track full-timers, then the figures drop below 50 percent. If we then add the graduate employees teaching classes, the true figure for FTTT faculty drops even lower.

Currently, there are over 1.2 million instructional faculty and staff, not even including the omissions noted above. College teachers are now one of the larger occupational groups. Nearly half (44%) are part-time, nearly all of these (95%) are non–tenure track. When the FTNTT are added in, that makes well over half a million teachers. The trends have been clear and fundamentally unchanged since the 1970s, except for the increasing percentage of FTNTT appointments in the last fifteen years.

So who are these new majority faculty? Unfortunately, the best figures look at only FT-PT comparisons and therefore lump full-time contingents in with their tenure track colleagues. Unlike the FTTT, who are mostly male, contingents are over half women. The gender balance varies by discipline, with disciplines with the most women, such as English composition, often having the most contingents. Women are concentrated in the lower portions of higher education, community college and adult non-credit instruction, where the contingent percentage is also greatest. Ironically, most college students are now women.

While there is no substantial overall difference in race or ethnicity between contingent (85% white) and FTTT (80% white), some job markets, both geographically and by discipline, have differentials. The figures, as with women, reveal a continuing pattern of under representation in the higher education faculty pool as a whole. The tradition of the uneven playing field with different starting lines continues to be reflected here.

With an average seniority in their current job of nearly seven years, compared to twelve for full-timers, most part-timers are not people who teach for a semester or two on their way to a tenure track job. My personal experience in many institutions is that most turnover among part-time contingents is in the first one to three semesters, and after that the workforce is much more stable. Stability is also increased by unionization, which usually brings with it some degree of job security and better compensation. With over six years' experience, most part-timers would qualify for tenure if it were available to them.

Contingents are less likely to be organized into unions, but a substantial number are represented. Full-time faculty are 37 percent union represented and part-time faculty are 29 percent. These percentages are both overstatements, especially for contingents, due to the exclusions noted above. Clearly, contingents are less likely to be organized, but a substantial number are represented. Compared with most contingent workers in the United States, contingent faculty are among the most unionized.

Pay and Total Income: With the average part-timer having a total personal income from all sources of only $52,500 ($12,100 from teaching) it disputes the notion that most part-timers are well-paid professionals who lend their expertise to academia for their own pleasure or as a favor to the educational enterprise. Most need their teaching income, and 31 percent work in more than one academic institution and 73 percent have other employment of some sort, with only 31 percent of full-timers having other employment. Again, these figures overstate part-timers' income because of database omissions. Unfortunately, the figures are only averages, which can be skewed by a few high-income earners. By comparison, full-timers averaged $81,200 total income, with all except $8,800 coming from their institution.

The other important aspect of pay is *pay rate*, not just total received. The only survey ever done, in 1999 by the Coalition on the Academic Workforce, a group of organizations representing various academic disciplines, found that most part-timers were working for less than $2,500 per three-credit course. Such a one-semester course usually requires three hours in class a week plus another six or more spent on preparation, office hours for students, course preparation, grading of student work, composing tests, and administrative requirements. This does not include the time spent planning the course before the semester begins. Part-timers who have kept careful time logs have reported that, when all time is counted, they often made less than $10 per hour, excluding their commute time to multiple jobs.

In teaching institutions a full-time load is considered to be three to five classes, or twenty-seven to forty-five hours per week. In fact, the difference between the number of classes taught (at one time in one school) by the average part-timer (2.4) and the average full-timer (3.3) is quite small. This is because FTTT faculty are expected to do departmental and committee work and often research and administrative work that part-timers are not. The difference in pay for the actual teaching work is striking. Though exact figures have never been compiled nationally, the majority of part-timers are working for half pay per course ($2,500) compared to their full-time colleagues ($5,000), in straight dollars that do not include other benefits that full-timers receive.

Degrees and Credentials: Most part-timers have less formal education than full-timers, with 67 percent of full-timers having Ph.D.'s or the equivalent against 27 percent of part-timers, though many part-timers are in graduate school while teaching. What these figures do not reveal is that a generation or two ago, the percentage of full-timers with Ph.D.'s would have been much less. As the size of the higher education workforce has increased, the percentage of those hired off the tenure track has also increased. A key difference is that this increase has come as people without doctoral degrees who, a generation before, would have been hired tenure track and then encouraged to get a Ph.D. later are now being hired on a contingent basis indefinitely. Therefore tenure track positions (called "lines"), now under 40 percent, are now the exception and are often viewed as an elite reward conferred only upon a minority of Ph.D.'s. Many FTTT faculty have admitted to me privately that if on the job market today, they would not have the qualifications demanded by the hiring committee on which they serve. In community colleges, the Ph.D. has become the degree of choice for prestige reasons even though most of the senior faculty have only master's degrees and research is not part of the job.

Are Part-Timers Professional Educators?

Part-time faculty are 92 percent teaching faculty, as compared to full-timers (only 70 percent), and especially compared to tenure track faculty, who often have research and administrative duties. Contrary to some stereotypes, most part-timers are professional educators, but with multiple jobs, often as K–12 teachers. An unknown number are simply unable to make a full living as educators, even though they wish to, and work in other vocations out of necessity.

Although the focus of this analysis is teaching, faculty research work is also being converted to casualized staff. Especially in the sciences, temporary, year-by-year postdoctoral research appointments are common, not just for a year or so upon graduation as before, but as a continuing way of life. More and more new Ph.D.'s are chasing relatively fewer FTTT faculty jobs and being hired as lower-paid contingents in the meantime.

How We Do Our Work: Despite our inferior pay and job security, we generally don't cut many of the educational corners we might be expected to. We are no more likely to retreat to multiple-choice machine-scored tests, instead of time-consuming essays, than full-time teachers. Many of us keep office hours for free and give out our home phone numbers to students. Nearly a quarter of us part-timers are still finding time to do research or creative work, even though we are not being paid for it. Clearly, we are doing professional quality work, albeit under unprofessional conditions.

Good Work But a Bad Living

The most significant of our unprofessional conditions is our contingency. To put it bluntly the employer's flexibility is our uncertainty. In externalizing the employment cost relationship to us, the advantage to the employer is obvious, especially now, faced with increasing numbers of nontraditional and part-time students whose enrollment patterns are progressively more difficult to predict and more sensitive to the state of the economy. Less obvious and more important are the ways those costs are paid by contingent faculty.

We lose income when we have to turn down jobs because schedules conflict or because we cannot predict employment or maximize employment opportunities. Income may also be lost due to instability as one person's contingent employment impacts all other members of a household in terms of planning their own personal and work lives.

Yet another way we bear the cost is by the absence or inadequacy of health insurance or health care, or the delaying of health care until health insurance can be reacquired. This obviously not only affects contingent faculty but all members of their families.

Besides the instability of income and health insurance coverage, the very fact of contingency exacts other more subtle costs. When one cannot be sure from one semester to the next of a work schedule, domestic duties like child care, shopping, cooking, elder care, and housework can rapidly become insurmountable problems, requiring a level of collective planning and organization in families that few are fully equipped to meet.

The status of contingency can also destroy social life. Between the limited income and the unstable and frequently odd hours, maintaining a "life," complete with recreation, personal development, and the cultivation of private relationships, can become extremely difficult. Many of our friends and relatives, when they get their first view, however partial, into the life we lead, reasonably ask, "Why do you keep doing it? Why don't you get a life?" While the question can be asked in one sentence, the answer is really the rest of this book. The one line answer might be, "Because it is good work that I love, but a bad living, which we are trying to make better."

Contingency limits our professional horizons. Recent research has shown that contingent work in academia, after two or three years, is not viewed as "positive experience" when one applies for permanent academic work, but rather is viewed as a detriment, increasing with the number of years that one has done it. It is "toiling for piece rates and accumulating deficits," to quote Kathleen Barker. When combined with the pervasive age discrimination (hidden under the desirability of "recency" of education or degree), contingent employment becomes dead-end day labor. Longtime contingents are often seen as "damaged" goods" when full-time tenure track positions are filled. Attempts to remedy this at bargaining tables, by proposing preference for FTTT jobs, have generally met stiff employer resistance.

Yet another aspect of the professional constriction faced by contingent faculty is that the time and energy it takes to maintain a living at contingent academic employment, or at contingent employment outside academia, leaves no time for developing the academic capital that can keep us attractive on the job market. The world of peer-reviewed journals, academic conferences, professional networks, updated personal references, possibilities for co-authorship, or even access to research libraries and facilities, are for the vast majority basically precluded.

However, the costs of the externalization of flexibility by academic employers do not end here. It turns out that the more we work, the greater the percentage of our time at work is hidden, unpaid, and not counted statistically. Here is how it plays out: if you primarily teach full-time at one college, you commute once. You can pick your place of residence in relation to your sole employment and other personal considerations, thereby minimizing your commute and possibly minimizing other trips of a personal nature. You also minimize your professional time outside of class, since you only have one set of administrators, one set of regulations, one place to turn in grades, one system of clerical and technical support to relate to, one parking lot, one office, one computer, one e-mail, voice-mail, and mailbox to check, one set of keys, one calendar to relate to, one set of student regulations and grade and transfer requirements to become familiar with in advising students, one set of syllabi to submit, one set of portfolios to create—if that is required to maintain or upgrade your employment status, and a single format of everything that as a faculty member you need to create to do your job. Virtually all contingent faculty face multiples of this, even if their total number of classes is the same or less than that of their FTTT colleagues. Most contingents teach at more than one place, have other paid work outside academia, or have serious unpaid responsibilities equivalent to another job.

And the more we work, the more of our time is absorbed by these activities. None of this time is counted as work hours by any of the standard administrative or economic indicators, but it comes out of people's lives just the same. This is all in addition to the concrete economic expense that most contingent faculty have of maintaining an office in the home and all the overhead associated with that, since they cannot rely on permanently having an office at all, and often cannot be in it during many of the hours that it might be useful anyway.

The stress associated with juggling all of these balls is hard to quantify, but all of us feel it. This stress degrades our personal and work relationships and gets in the way of collective action as well. This stress problem is a dissertation in social psychology just waiting to be written, though the grant money might be hard to find.

A final aspect of management's externalization of the cost of flexibility onto the contingent faculty is the exploitation of our commitment to our job and our students. In trying to do a good job, we render a professional commitment, including unpaid departmental work, and receive unprofessional wages and little respect, except from our students. This dynamic is also used to discipline contingent faculty. Employers imply that if one behaves "professionally," one has a greater chance of being rehired, or even possibly hired into a FTTT position. This pressure to act like a full professional naturally exacts a psychological toll as well.

Perhaps the iron recognition of this reality can be found in the series of columns by Jill Carroll in the *Chronicle of Higher Education*, which has finally taken notice of the contingent majority. However, the *Chronicle* has chosen to focus on these issues through the eyes of a Texas part-timer who describes in her regular column all of the compromises, hustles, and gimmicks that contingent faculty use to put together a minimal living. (i.e., "Don't spend more than ten minutes on one paper.") Unfortunately, she describes them from the point of view that explicitly argues that broader change in conditions is fundamentally impossible, however attractive it might be.

How Our Class Position Has Changed

Conditions of contingent faculty in general have declined radically as our numbers have grown. Before 1970, there were a few community professionals teaching specialized courses, supplemented, especially in the community colleges and adult education programs, by full-time public school teachers working evenings. Not only were they a small minority of the faculty, they were often paid at the same rate per course as tenured teachers and received many of the same conditions of work. These folks were generally hired because of special expertise or to fill a temporary shortage in a discipline, not primarily for cost savings or for schedule flexibility.

Just as we have become the majority of the faculty, our conditions have worsened; as a further irony most of us now depend upon our contingent faculty work as an essential part of our total income. These trends have created a new class line within higher education institutions. This class line is not between contingent and regular faculty—though the difference between them has increased in some ways—but rather, as contingent faculty have become the norm for faculty, between contingent faculty and those who own, control, and manage institutions of higher education in the United States. This change, of course, has also affected full-time faculty. The key point here is that the majority of college faculty have become professional skilled wage workers as compared to the traditional full-time tenure track faculty, who were partly wage workers but also partly independent professionals with their tenure, professional discretion, and governance powers in the institutions. A similar transition took place among public school teachers a hundred years ago as they were transformed from independent schoolmasters to the waged workers of the mass system of public education. The rise of teacher unionism in the early 1900s was the conscious response of teachers to that change.

We faculty, mostly contingent, are now mainly workers and are often one of the largest numerical groups of workers employed in academia. We retain a contradictory class position for a variety of reasons. Also, in common with most other contingent workers, our class position, and certainly our class perception, is heavily influenced by the class position of our spouses and other family members who may have more secure economic positions outside the working class.

Another source of contradiction in the class position is that many of us do not have working class origins. Here there are parallels with other groups whose entry into the American (waged) working class was from non-working class origins, such as the rural immigrants to the factories of the cities in the late nineteenth and early twentieth centuries, whether from rural America, especially the South and Midwest, or from Europe, Asia, or Latin America. What those people all had in common was the rural-to-urban transition and also, in many cases, the transition from peasant to wage labor in an industrial society. For many, this constituted a lateral or even upward move in class location. For our contingent faculty, we are often moving downward out of some section of the middle classes, even if our formal education is greater than our parents. We must remember this history as we try to construct a plan to organize our colleagues.

Just as many of us are economically less well off than our parents, the power we have on our jobs is less than our colleagues of yore. Academic power relations have altered as the organizational structure of higher education has changed. Many of those considered by higher administration as "faculty" are, to us, "bosses." This large sector of full-time tenure track faculty officeholders sees itself and is seen by others as "faculty," but in their role as department heads, lead faculty, coordinators, program directors, and assistant deans, they are seen by contingent faculty as the employer. The casual nature of the employment relationship that has been constructed in higher education has also been accompanied by decentralization of authority and practice of hiring, scheduling, evaluation, assignment, and firing of contingent faculty. Since these administrators/faculty perform all these functions for contingent faculty, they are objectively "bosses".

This decentralization of higher education has reached such a point in many institutions that if administrators are asked directly how many contingent faculty are actually employed, what they are doing, what they are being paid, what the personal employment history is, they often respond with the academic version of "Huh?" For this reason, all figures related to contingent faculty, which almost always come from institutional administrations, must be taken with the greatest caution. The lack of accurate statistical data is in fact a major characteristic of this casualized employment relationship, of this workforce itself, and is a major consideration in organizing strategy.

This phenomenon has also led large sections of the full-time faculty, even those without supervisory responsibility, to take the same subjective attitude as central administrators ("hands off" and "see no evil") toward contingent faculty. This is perhaps a major reason for the relative slowness of the national faculty unions in grappling with the strategic implications of the growth of contingent faculty. There is no need to assume malice, or even selfishness, to explain this. The invisibility of these transitions, and of contingent faculty, may be explanation enough.

Our Supervisors: Contingent faculty are not the only ones in higher education whose class location is changing and contradictory. Pressure has grown to abolish elected department heads and simultaneously assign administrative duties to regular faculty, in piecemeal fashion. Top management has increased the ranks of the full-time middle management, academic professionals, and their support staffs. The inhabitants of slots labeled "department head," "assistant dean, or "program director" have found themselves torn by their contradictory imperatives as their percentage grows. From the point of view of contingent faculty, being managed, hired, and fired by those who themselves occupy a contradictory class location, is no gift at all. Since many of these supervisors still see themselves primarily as faculty, and often as progressives, they frequently play the role of supervisor in an ambivalent and incompetent way. They pretend to be colleagues but act like bosses. These supervisors tend to minimize the time spent on their supervisory duties and then react defensively when questioned by subordinates. In some programs and disciplines, such as composition and English as a second language, it is common that supervisors themselves are contingent non-tenure track.

When faced with collective action, many of these faculty supervisors feel personally betrayed and develop generalized hostility. This reaction has perhaps been most extreme when graduate employees organize because it highlights their dual role of employer and administration agent as well as academic mentor and professor. The tension is heightened by the increased use of contingent faculty and the declining percentage of full-time tenured faculty. If that weren't enough, many full-time tenured faculty are finding their own position degraded. They are having to do work formerly shared with other FTTT colleagues whose numbers are declining, and they are finding their own traditional prerogatives of such benefits as administrative support, supplies, research money, time off, and scheduling preferences being limited. Additionally, some full-time faculty have actually been confronted with the possible loss of tenure altogether (University of Minnesota and Bennington College), which has sparked among them some of the most substantial collective activity since the early days of faculty collective bargaining in the 1970s.

The Other Big Losers: Students and Society

The main cost of all these changes is not even borne by the individual teacher, who survives or leaves the profession, but by the larger community and society. For every scintilla of flexibility the employer gains, contingent faculty members lose it and become less able to manage and plan their own lives. The casualization of this and the increased work and commute time is a crucial element in the decline of voluntary organizations and general citizenship behavior of all sorts.

As Paul Loeb details in *Soul of a Citizen*, no one can count how many community meetings, churches, political clubs, neighborhood associations, sports leagues, fraternal groups, PTAs, social groups, and, yes, trade unions themselves, have been weakened and even extinguished by the loss of voluntary time and energy by large numbers of their potential members and leaders. This loss is particularly true of working-class people and is one more indication of how college teaching has become a more working-class job. We have less time to voluntarily help, socialize with, and get to know one another. Society as a whole and the public quality of life are losing many of the potential contributions of some of the most highly trained and motivated workers and citizens.

The direct impact upon students can perhaps best be summarized by the commonly used slogan, "Faculty teaching conditions are student learning conditions." Students register blindly for a course taught by "TBA" or "Staff." They cannot easily meet with faculty outside class and often cannot find a teacher after the term is finished. There is limited communication with the faculty and almost none of the informal relaxed student-teacher time so important to college life and learning. Some researchers and administrators have asserted that contingents are actually poorer teachers, but the research has been far from conclusive on this point. What is clear is that it is a much greater struggle for contingent faculty to do their job well than it is for their FTTT colleagues. The reason for this difference is generally invisible to most students, but when they are made aware of the situation, they have often responded with great support for struggles to change these inequities.

2

Contingent Faculty Organizing

Now that we have a broad picture of the terrain on which contingent faculty must live and work, it is time to discuss what we can do to change it. I say "we" purposely, because I am now inviting you, the reader, to join me and many others in the movement to change the conditions of contingency and thereby change all of higher education—and perhaps the labor movement itself in the process. In general, organizing is all about getting people together to feel more hope than fear and fatalism about the prospect of change in their lives. But in order to organize, we have to have a *strategy*.

Easier said than done. Developing and following an overall plan of action is essential for any group that wants to make permanent social change. In organizing workers, any strategy must revolve around two basic considerations. The "objective" factors, the material realities of the workplace and the power relations within it and the "subjective" factors, how the actors, individually and collectively, think and behave now and how they might be led to think and behave under active organizing conditions. The line between these two is not always firm, but conceptually these are the two categories that create and re-create the terrain upon which organizing occurs. Any strategy for change through organizing has to start with a consideration of both.

Material Conditions and Power Relations
My central argument is that the new majority faculty is a group that has experienced proletarianization in nearly all of its classical components: declining wages and job security, loss of ancillary compensation, loss of autonomy and control of the work process, and, finally, loss of the (professional) perquisites that have traditionally gone along with the work of a (tenured) college teacher. This has been accompanied by the splitting of full-time jobs in two ways: by simply cutting them into smaller pieces, i.e., a three- or four- or five-class full-time load parceled

out as one or two class assignments to adjuncts and the unbundling of the various faculty tasks so that these adjuncts are mainly teachers, playing no role in the research, service, and governance aspects of the institution. This second type of splitting can reach down as far as selection of textbooks, definition of acceptable class size, printing limitations, and classroom assignments. Just as over one hundred years ago Frederick Winslow Taylor's "scientific management" brought greater division of labor and more intense supervision to manufacturing, current higher education administrators seek to "unbundle" the traditional tasks of professors for economic advantage and managerial power.

Consciousness: How Our Colleagues Think

As individuals being thrust full bore into the working class and at the same time often facing downward mobility, in aspiration if not always in material reality, contingent faculty naturally exhibit a dual consciousness and behavior. On the one hand, our years of graduate education have instilled in us a belief in individual merit, the "Protestant work ethic," and higher education's version of the Horatio Alger myth: Work hard and smart and you will succeed. Throughout this education we are close to well-compensated faculty whom we wish to emulate. This intensifies our beliefs and leads us to pursue, sometimes for years and even decades, the search for individual solutions and recognition of our "merit."

This contradiction between our current reality and societally imposed hopes can be called "mixed consciousness." Many of us initially retain the individualism of the striver, while at the same time attempting to struggle against what we perceive as individual unfairness directed against us and frustrating our ability to achieve recognition. One minute we may be kowtowing most obsequiously to administrators and FTTT faculty and at the next privately expressing murderous feelings toward those very same individuals. Although this doesn't constitute a particularly useful building block for organizing, understanding its genesis can provide an organizer the tools to help transform a primitive and individual rebelliousness into something collective. Since it arises from fundamentally conditions, this consciousness can be changed into support for collective action, although it is always susceptible to backsliding when isolation takes hold.

Finally, the objective fact that we are now workers allows us to join the world of the broader labor movement, and most of our students who are working-class people themselves. Most college faculty unionism in the past has been dominated by the somewhat insular "guild consciousness" of the skilled professional seeking to protect existing privileges. This new situation for most college teachers could be the basis for the rise of a new, more expansive, working-class consciousness and a new social unionism among faculty. It also could lead to new and deeper relationships with our students, giving us the ability to say to them, "We workers...." The potential power of this new relationship between college students and their teachers could help to transform higher education pedagogically, politically, and economically.

Our Full-time Tenured and Tenure Track Colleagues (FTTT)

Just as we contingent faculty have had our material position and our consciousness changed in the last thirty years, so have full-time tenure track faculty and administrators. FTTT faculty are coming to occupy a deeply anomalous position. On the one hand, the 1980 Supreme Court decision in a case involving Yeshiva University declared private university professors to be managers. On the other hand, there has been a gradual degradation of their employment situation, even as they have become a "privileged minority" of faculty. The exceptions to this rule, namely the faculty stars in a few departments at Research I universities, are merely the exceptions of the employment situation of most FTTT faculty, which is most potently symbolized by the continuing attacks on tenure.

Universities: At the same time that contingent faculty numbers have been increasing, an evolution has taken place among the full-time tenure track faculty in almost all sectors of higher education. At the research universities, this has meant greatly increasing publishing requirements; raising the bar for hiring, promotion, and tenure; and putting the pressure on the less well-known faculty to teach more, though that pressure has often been successfully resisted. The overall loss of full-time tenured positions at research universities has meant that departmental curricular work and other collective business is split among fewer hands. So those who are not "stars," despite their relatively elite status, have found their traditional conditions threatened.

Research FTTT faculty duties have altered further from academic mentor to supervisor with the increasing use of grad employees as both teachers and researchers, which become particularly uncomfortable for some faculty when grad employees have tried to unionize. In some universities FTTT faculty have been open allies of the grad employees. But the vast majority has been neutral or hostile with only a few openly standing with the grad employees, such as at Yale.

Non–Ph.D granting universities that traditionally focused on teaching have begun to require more research without necessarily decreasing teaching loads. Committees of these institutions are passing on the hiring, promotion, and tenure of applicants even though a majority of the committee could not pass the bar themselves. The culture of academic competition has permeated these institutions as formerly "urban comprehensive universities" or ex-teachers' colleges strive to become "world class" universities. Again, the result for "non-star" FTTT faculty is more pressure and higher research demands—ironically at the same time that tuition-driven schools are pushing to increase class size and thereby effectively increase teaching loads.

Liberal Arts Colleges: The private liberal arts colleges seem to have been impacted the least by these changes, but externally the environment in which they function has become much more hostile to the traditional market they occupy. So, while liberal arts colleges have hired fewer contingents and have altered the work of their full-time tenure track faculty less, many have simply collapsed, through bankruptcy or merger, or radically transformed themselves in an attempt to adapt to the new market realities. This trend accelerated in the 1970s, with religion-based liberal arts colleges in small towns throughout the country changing ownership, bankrupting, merging, or otherwise transforming. Parsons College in Iowa, now Maharishi University, is one of the most famous. Some of these former liberal arts colleges have become mini-empires running classes in many states, as they imitate the for-profits such as the University of Phoenix. Many of these institutional changes, such as satellites on public community college campuses, have brought with them many more contingent faculty.

Community Colleges: In the community colleges, full-time faculty members are today almost always a minority of the total faculty. Entire departments have been reduced to a full-time department chair managing a flock of part-timers. Institutions in which department chairmanships were never highly coveted, generally only giving partial release time from teaching and little if any increased pay, this new situation has resulted in administrative conscription of chairs, on rotational or name-in-the-hat basis, under the threat that if existing full-timers did not "pull their weight," their whole department would be consolidated with another or leadership would be imposed upon them. At the same time, there has been an elimination of departments as arenas for democratic

California Debates What Is Faculty Work

A potent discussion of the difference between the contingent faculty and the full-time tenured faculty has been occurring in California community colleges, over the question: "What percentage of a full-time faculty members' total work is constituted by the teaching and other duties that part-time (contingent) faculty members do?" The answer guided the local allocation of the pay equity money placed in the state budget in 2001. This debate has been conducted in every single community college district in the state through the union-management collective bargaining process, and the percentages ended up ranging from the 60 to 100. Some are not yet decided.

Of course, community college full-time faculty do not have the same duties as faculty in four-year schools, so this will not be the final word in the equity discussion. However, this debate opens discussions that, depending on how they are pursued, can be positive or negative for the future of higher education and for contingent faculty organizing. Positively, it forces open discussion of all the tasks that contingent faculty are conducting as part of their instructional duties, thereby creating pressure for their compensation. Negatively, however, this debate supports the administrative thrust to unbundle faculty work by focusing on the potential to divide and parcel out the work of curriculum development, instructional delivery, evaluation, and individual student contact such as tutoring and advising. All of these have traditionally been packaged in the person of the individual faculty member, whose norms have been developed collectively by faculty. So, the results could make things better, or worse. That's why it's important, and why it has been a major subject on contingent faculty listservs in California.

faculty governance and collective academic decision making. In many community colleges today, the word *department* is merely an archaic disciplinary colloquialism with no official administrative meaning.

Thus increasing pressure on the average full-time community college faculty member to teach more and larger classes, serve on more committees, spend more time on collective departmental business, and perform more semi-administrative functions, despite the continuing growth of administrative staff. The loss of full-time disciplinary colleagues has also meant the loss of the collegiality. All this has occurred while FTTT faculty have been aging and the general level of per-student tax support has been shrinking. The result has been a drop in morale, individually and collectively, such that few who knew community colleges in the 1960s and early 1970s would fully recognize them today.

Implications for Our Organizing: This is now a complicated calculus, for while in some ways the difference between the FTTT faculty and contingent faculty is greater than ever, in other ways the forces acting upon both groups have created the basis for a firm alliance. If present trends continue, we will see a convergence in the conditions of the two groups, but it will be a convergence of the casualized, the de-skilled, and the insecure. Only a few faculty at the top will hold professor or consultant status and be making decisions that traditionally were made collectively by all FTTT faculty.

How the two groups respond to these changes will have implications for organizing contingent faculty. If most FTTT see the danger of job loss or job degradation as converging with the contingent majority, then new openings for faculty unionism will be available. If, on the other hand, the majority of FTTT faculty respond to these conditions by looking for individual solutions, such as counting the days until their own retirement, seeking to become a "star," pursuing administrative advancement, and focusing upon developing outside consulting businesses related to their discipline, then the potential for alliance will decrease and the potential collective power to defend FTTT positions for the future will decline as well. The attack on tenure is merely the most obvious example of an administration strategically responding to these changes. Administrators also wave the carrot as well as the stick in encouraging individual responses—with early retirement packages, administrative positions, and the rewarding (even requiring) of outside entrepreneurial behavior (including grants and corporate contracts). Administrators also encourage faculty unions to bargain multiple tiers ("selling the unhired"), by creating further degraded conditions for not-yet-hired FTTT faculty. That most faculty unions are led by the senior FTTT cohort has allowed this tactic to be effective.

"At Will" Employment and the Social Contract: Unlike most "developed" nations, in the United States most employees who do not have union representation function under the "at will" common law doctrine. What this means is that there is no legal restriction upon the employers to keep them from dismissing employees for any reason or no reason and with no notice or explanation. The exceptions to this, which cover only a minority of the workforce, are 1) union contracts with "just cause" discipline and discharge provisions; 2) public employment with civil service due process discipline and discharge protections; 3) civil rights laws forbidding discrimination against protected groups (race, sex, color, national origin, religion, veteran status, and, in some localities, sexual orientation—but these can be difficult to enforce); 4) retaliation for exercise of rights under various labor and employment laws (National Labor Relations Act, OSHA, FMLA, etc.); and 5) legally enforceable tenure regulations for traditional FTTT faculty. While this list of protections has expanded over the years, the practical ability of most workers to enforce these laws without union support has always been limited due to costs and fear of retaliation.

However, since the Second World War, the labor management "pact" has created the social expectation, at least in the primary labor market for which standards largely set by industrial union contracts, that regular jobs would be full-time, include benefits, living wages, and carry the expectation of continued employment as long as work was adequately performed and the employer did not experience an economic crisis. Temporary seasonal or emergency layoffs may occur, but employer and employee relationship was seen by both as ongoing and having some permanence. For agreeing to this, employers received labor peace, policed by unions who signed multi-year contracts and did not question the general outlines of corporate or government policy. The fact that this social expectation had virtually no legal standing in non-union private workplaces did not make it any less real there, either. The destruction of that relationship, legally supported or otherwise, is much of the story behind the changes in the U.S. workforce since the 1970s. In application to higher education, where this expectation was legally enforceable through tenure statutes, case law, and union contracts, the change has been somewhat more gradual.

If enough of the remaining FTTT faculty and the organizations they lead can be convinced that the future of higher education lies with an active alliance with contingent faculty and their organizations, then the future of the struggle is much brighter. The answer will probably be mixed, with more FTTT community college faculty making the alliance decision than those in the most prestigious realms of higher education. In either case, our main goal should be to build our movement in whatever way we can, largely independently if we must and in alliance with FTTT faculty if we can. Our ability to build our own movement is what will mainly determine how most FTTT faculty line up.

Administrators' Perspectives and Vulnerabilities

In most cases outside community colleges, administrators serve on behalf of an appointed board of trustees, drawn mainly from business. In an economically counter-cyclical industry, such as in most of non-elite higher education, administrators may feel a certain pressure to let the bottom line lead institutional policy. Non-elite higher education is a counter-cyclical industry in the sense that the demand (need) for its product (education) grows in periods of recession and depression—just those times when funding for the institution either through government appropriations or voluntary donations is likely at its lowest. Likewise, in good economic times, more potential students are likely to find living-wage jobs and therefore delay their higher education aspirations. This phenomenon has become both more pronounced and more important. Since the 1970s college students are drawn increasingly from working adults rather than new high school graduates. This inherent condition of the "industry" has always produced pressure on administrators to pay attention to the short-term economics of their enterprise, but in the post–World War Two boom, there was enough money coming to the system to sustain growth even in times of recession.

What changed for administrators in the 1970s is what is called in the private sector "the profit crisis"; in higher education it's a "budget crisis." The attempt to prosecute the unpopular Vietnam War on the basis of government borrowing, while at the same time not raising taxes or sharply reducing public services, resulted in a lessening of economic growth and rising prices, the heretofore-capitalist impossibility of "stagflation." In higher education this resulted in more nontraditional students, many veterans and women reentering the workforce, literally banging on the doors of higher education as disposable institutional income was shrinking. Administrators responded to this problem, sometimes reluctantly, by hiring legions of contingent faculty and also cutting costs in other ways (larger class sizes, deferred maintenance, contracting out of non-instructional services and seeking educational contracts outside the institution, i.e., "contracting in"). Some institutions hired virtually no full-time faculty, except in growing occupational fields, for a decade or more.

The net result of these pressures opened that generation of administrators (and trustees) to traditional corporate management models to solve their problems. As that generation of administrators retired, many college presidents and boards of trustees replaced the retirees with people directly from the corporate sector, figuring that if the problem was parallel to that of corporate management, why should the institution pay for on-the-job retraining of academics when you could hire people with corporate management experience who were ready to go "just in time"? Thus, in the twentieth-first century, we have many more educational institutions run by people who have not only taught very little but who do not see themselves primarily as educators, even rhetorically, and who much prefer to be labeled CEOs than to bear the burden of "educational leadership."

Who Are the Activists?

Activists do come in all shapes and sizes, but some are more likely to come forward than others. Thus a major strategic consideration in organizing contingent faculty is the rise in the number of women in the academy. This occurred just as women were becoming less likely to see themselves as wanting only part-time or contingent employment, but rather confronting their professional and economic need to support themselves and others. The combination of the economic demands of large numbers of women and their rising aspirations and the movement for equality against traditional gender discrimination in higher education has meant that women have often been the leading activists. Even more often women have been the majority of strong supporters of organizations struggling both for better pay and conditions in contingent jobs and for fair and preferential access to full-time jobs, especially in the fields dominated by contingent faculty, such as English Composition and English as a Second Language (ESL).

However, no disciplines are uniformly hostile to organizing. Even business departments, where one might expect to find the headquarters of ideological anti-unionism, have turned out in practice, at least among contingent faculty, to include many who recognize that they need an organization even if they have a management background and are ambivalent about "joining the labor movement." It does remain true, however, that those fields in which the fewest alternative well-paid and secure employment opportunities exist outside the academy are those that have produced a disproportionate percentage of activists. It's the rare organizing committee that does not include folks from English and ESL, other humanities, and some social scientists. However, vocational program faculty are often among the most serious activists, since many jobs they come from pay so much better than contingent teaching.

Another characteristic of the activists is that they tend to be people without Ph.D.'s and from less prestigious institutions. It is rare, though not unheard of, for an Ivy League Ph.D. to lead an organizing drive among contingent faculty. This may change as more new Ph.D's have experience with grad employee unions. A little reasonable speculation might be useful, however. One possibility is that people with only a master's degree are more likely to have mixed in their graduate classes with folks from unionized professions: public school teachers, nurses, social workers, etc. People with doctorates are more likely to have mixed in their classes largely with people from elite backgrounds, with little past contact with unions except perhaps as supervisors. Another possibility is that people who ended their education, at least temporarily, with master's degrees are more likely to have some sort of union experience in their own personal and family backgrounds than those who have achieved the extra years of education necessary for a Ph.D. Another possibility is that Ph.D.'s are more likely to still believe that they personally can achieve individual upward mobility ("grab the brass ring") by snaring a full-time tenure track position. This would hold especially true for those from elite institutions.

In my experience, African-American, Latino, and other people of color tend to be more supportive of organizing. This is hardly surprising, given that unionization in any job has tended to increase the equality of treatment and pay. Just as contingent faculty in general are the faculty who most need an organization, those who have historically and presently been victims of discrimination need the modicum of fairness and collective power that a decent union can bring. However, within this generalization, workers who have the most to lose are sometimes very fearful of putting it at risk through becoming activists, especially if they do not have close ties with the initial organizers. Add to this the fears of many immigrants and others on visas that drawing attention to themselves could put themselves or family members at risk. The grad employee union movement has had to grapple with this issue because of the large percentage of foreign graduate students. Those most successful have found that international students can often become leading activists, but only if they feel their particular issues are being addressed and they feel support and protection sufficient to overcome their fears.

People who are the first generation of their families to have college or advanced-degree education, no matter what their background, may at first feel privileged to be working in higher education. However, partly because of their own working-class backgrounds, they may later become key activists once they realize that they need not hide their own personal history but find it a source of pride in the movement. When working-class academics come "out of the closet," they can bring an essential experience and commitment to the fight for equity.

The lesson herein is that the initial group of activists, if not already mixed in all ways, needs to make a special effort at the very start of their activity to create a group at least representative of the whole contingent faculty. This means mixed by discipline as well as personal background. The ultimate success of the whole effort may be determined by this factor. If the organizing effort comes to be seen as white, or male, or representing solely those in the humanities and social sciences, a hostile administration will exploit those weaknesses to divide and destroy.

My years in the movement and this research have convinced me that those most likely to get involved are those most committed to the job. This can be because they are freeway flyers who only teach for a living and therefore feel the inequities in a particularly personal way. It can be any person who is particularly committed to education and the teaching process, even if she does not personally teach for her main income. Both groups are well represented and exist in all disciplines. Further, I have found that people who do this work for more than a couple of years are much more likely to become activists. Unfortunately, we are also more likely to be psychologically and physically damaged by the experience by the time we become activists. Years without respect, material or professional, makes people angry and less self-confident. Many of us have found the answer to both problems in the collective struggle, especially if there is at least one other person to link closely with who has some past experience and a broader perspective.

The Message: Respect

As one old union organizer said, ultimately all organizing revolves around a demand for respect: respect for the people who are doing the work and respect for the work that they are doing. Perhaps the most famous union slogan came from the 1968 Memphis AFSCME (American Federation of State, County and Municipal Employees) African-American sanitation workers strike. "I Am a Man," it read. Their struggle for respect, which included living wages and safe conditions, inspired and mobilized millions in their support, including Martin Luther King Jr., who gave his life in that struggle.

The aphorism about respect certainly holds true for contingent faculty. Each time an FTTT teacher or administrator uses the word *faculty* to refer only to the FTTT, one more piece of grit is ground into the eye of any contingent within earshot. The list of disrespectful and inequitable irritations could fill this page: new parking tags needed every year; limits on copying, library access, recreation facilities; lack of names in class schedules and catalogs, in phone books, on office doors; and no notices of college or departmental news or meetings. A useful organizing tactic can be to make a list in a meeting of all the examples of petty disrespect we face every term.

One seldom recognized aspect of the exploitation of contingent faculty is that in addition to doing the same work in the classroom as the FTTT faculty, we must also maintain "professorial behavior" despite our invisible status within the institution. This emotional work imposed upon us is draining because not only is it required but it is also completely unsupported and unacknowledged.[1] And this is just another way in which we are placed in a position of superexploiting ourselves in order to do our job. We cannot teach students successfully if we treat our students the way we are treated by our employers. If we did, little learning would take place and many students would exit the classroom.

This requirement also creates among us a kind of double-consciousness similar to what W.E.B. Du Bois described for African-Americans, who have to maintain a dual social face, one toward the white world of power and another toward the African-American community. In less extreme form, contingent faculty must maintain one face toward all who have or might have power over them and another face shared only among themselves. Although this phenomenon exists in all wage labor jobs, contingent faculty are an extreme case because of great contrast between the public perception of their status and the reality of their existence. The brittleness resulting from this state can cause contingent faculty to fear revelation of their true status to students for fear of losing respect and the ability to teach effectively. The same holds true for contingent faculty's relationships with people outside academia. Gappa and Leslie's book, *The Invisible Faculty*, was appropriately titled because contingent faculty are not only treated as invisible by administrators but are "in the closet" by our own actions, for perfectly rational although ultimately collectively self-limiting reasons. Just as the movement for gay rights allowed gay people to exit the closet individually, and so join a collective struggle for equality and social legitimization, so too the movement for contingent faculty equity allows some contingent faculty to come out of their closets to students, friends, and others. This often results in new allies and unexpected help as well as emotional support.

Specific Demands
While all organizing may be ultimately about respect, specific issues are obviously important. Thirty years of contingent faculty activism have given us some

observable patterns. Two central clusters of issues consistently emerge at the top of the priority list and symbolize for most contingent faculty the lack of respect we feel. These issue clusters cross the individual situations of contingent faculty.

The first is job security. This has two major subdivisions: the security of assignment, placement, and retention, priority for additional classes of the existing contingent workers over newer hires and preference for upgrading to full-time tenure track positions when they occur. The demands to cover job security and upgrading are seniority rights issues. While seniority systems are never perfect, it is still the best general system as a substitute for the arbitrary "standards" virtually all employers use in its absence. In academe, seniority systems might include college, department, discipline, or course seniority. One may have seniority for one's customary course load or, contrarily, round-robin seniority where all get one before anyone gets two classes. Seniority can be mitigated by factors such as "qualifications," personal specialization, affirmative action needs, scheduling demands, or performance evaluations. There can be seniority systems based on date of hire, first semester taught, total number of semesters taught, total classes or credits taught.

A minority of faculty are covered by seniority systems of sorts, called tenure. While important as a precedent and invaluable for those under them, current tenure systems have many negative aspects, among the worst is when it is treated as a gift or special reward, subject to gross political and personal manipulation, rather than a form of basic job security that all workers should be able to earn as a right. The core principle of seniority in education should be the recognition that work adequately performed in the past yields experience that, in general, leads to greater skill. This greater all-around and long-term efficiency of familiar and committed employees redounds to the benefit of the employer as well as the student.

That most employers strongly resist this demand points to a conclusion that most administrators actually are much less concerned with the quality of the education provided than they are with the danger that a more experienced, and hence perhaps rebellious or stubborn, workforce might challenge their "right" to manage in the context of restricted administrative flexibility. The administrative principle of "fresh blood" is often openly invoked. This is one more reason most contingent faculty have come to the unshakable conclusion that the people running the majority of higher education institutions today are not only ignorant of what goes on in classrooms but are in fact militantly agnostic about it, unless it generates student ("customers") complaints. The firmness of this general assessment by contingent faculty is surprising and strongly contradicts the still-common perception of FTTT faculty that administrators, even up to the president, are still "colleagues." This is one more example of the development of class consciousness among the new majority faculty. We are much closer to "defining the enemy" as a goal of education, to use Australian adult educator Mike Newman's expression.[2]

The second cluster of issues that inevitably arises is that of equal pay, compensation, and treatment for equal work. The notion of equity in this context is so deeply rooted in U.S. society that any labor educator or organizer can relate dozens of examples of conversations explaining that, "No, there really is no general equal-pay-for-equal-work law in this country, despite how obviously just the principle." All general legislative efforts in this direction, other than to protect specific groups from invidious discrimination, have been unsuccessful.

Even if it were fully mandated legally, the concept of equal pay for equal work is not a perfect principle. It fails to recognize inequality of need, inequality of effort, inequality of condition within which the work is performed, the inherent inability of any work to be exactly equal to any other. Nevertheless, this principle has exactly the same virtues, and thereby the same necessity, as the seniority demand. It is a restriction upon the capricious unfairness of employers, and it highlights the truly important principle of the right of all employees to equity and fair treatment. Highlighting this principle has the added advantage of drawing previously disparate individuals together in a collectivity that makes it possible for them to conduct joint discussions, act together for greater equity, and perhaps ultimately create compensation principles that go beyond equal pay for equal work. But the doorway of equal pay for equal work must be walked through on the way to anything more equitable. And the path beyond that doorway would have to lead to a post-capitalist alternative economy and society, in which a community of equals could democratically apportion resources and labor tasks and roles "to each according to their need."

These two clusters, job security and equity of compensation, should not be seen as primary universal demands for contingent faculty in all societies at all times but rather for our context in the current U.S. capitalist period. If, for instance, the social wage were higher in the United States as it is and has been in other countries, these issues might not matter as much as some others. If health care access were not tied to employment, the specific issue of job security would be less crucial. If no one were allowed by a comprehensive employment and welfare system to sink below a reasonable living standard even with temporary unemployment, job security would certainly be less important. If legal limits were placed upon rents and the prices of other essentials of life, pay levels and other direct individual compensation would be less important demands. But since the social wage in the United States is so uneven, so low, and falling, these two clusters of issues must be seen as the crucial demands now, just as they are for most contingent workers in the U.S. economy, right behind personal safety.

Competitive Unionism: Good, Bad, or Indifferent for Contingent Faculty?

With the rise of a movement among contingent faculty and the declining percentage and declining absolute number of FTTT faculty, it was probably inevitable that the national unions would become more interested in contingent faculty and that competition for bargaining units would ensue. We have the precedent of the American Federation of Teachers (AFT) vs. the National Education Association (NEA) representational wars in the public schools in the 1960s–1980s. Even for higher education contingent faculty, this has occurred before, most especially in places where the common pattern was combined contingent/FTTT units, such as in the public sector in California and New York. Now, however, we see union competition for contingent-only units. This includes the private sector, where the contingent faculty are safe from the roadblocks of the 1980 U.S. Supreme Court decision, *NLRB v. Yeshiva University*, which largely halted private sector FTTT faculty organizing in the 1980s by declaring FTTT faculty the managers of their institution.

As with most complicated and developing phenomena, a little history is necessary here. One of the earliest major recognized faculty bargaining units in higher education came in the City College of New York (now the City University of New York) system. That unit, perhaps unique in the United States, has come to include all FTTT faculty, all adjunct faculty, and all graduate employees (considered adjuncts at CUNY). From the late 1960s, this bargaining unit, represented by the Professional Staff Congress (PSC), AFT, has a peculiar history, which has exerted a great influence on the movement, because of its size and its placement in the nation's largest city. However, the pattern of placing graduate employees in a combined all-faculty unit has not been reproduced. The PSC faculty unit has always been led by FTTT faculty, who have also been major figures in the national AFT and hence in the national faculty union movement.

Another of the earliest faculty units organized was in the Chicago city colleges, also in the late 1960s, as an FTTT-only unit represented by the Cook

County College Teachers Union (CCCTU), AFT Local 1600. This unit likewise wielded considerable influence in the national faculty union movement, and its pattern of FTTT-only units has dominated patterns in the Midwest and much of the nation.

In California, in the huge community college and California state university systems (but not the University of California), the pattern, fought for by California Federation of Teachers in this case, has been to have combined unions with one union local representing both FTTT and contingent (of whom all are PT in the California community colleges) faculty. Furthermore, the pattern has been to have combined bargaining units with one collective bargaining contract covering both, with some sections applying only to one or the other faculty group. This has also been the general pattern in Washington State as well.

The major point is that until recently, the decision of which union would represent contingent faculty was generally made in conjunction with, usually subordinate to, the decision of which union would represent FTTT faculty. The contingent-only units that existed were the exceptions that proved the rule and existed either for very peculiar historic reasons or because of particularly obdurate and hostile local full-time faculty leadership. Most existing bargaining units nationally, however, were and are FTTT only, with the contingents unorganized.[3] This pattern has begun to change since 1998, and an increasing number of contingent-only bargaining units are forming. Thus, the potential for competition among major unions for representation rights in contingent faculty-only units is now greater than it once was..

The issue of whether to have various organizations competing to organize adjunct faculty has been debated on a number of contingent faculty listservs.[4] Therefore, I make no claim to originality for what follows, but I have tried to compile and evaluate them for purposes of a summary discussion.

Arguments against Competitive Unionism: Several arguments against competitive unionism exist. First, competition tends to confuse and demobilize people in the proposed bargaining unit because a major focus of the campaign inevitably becomes the competing unions' attributes. The net result is a lower level of rank-and-file contingent participation, a higher level of cynicism, and, ultimately, a weaker union coming out of the competitive election and attempting to negotiate a first contract. The very process of the competitive campaign tends to reduce the propaganda to a level of "what we can do for you" and the sale of a particular union as the better insurance agency rather than building a union of an activist workers' movement nurtured from the grass roots up to combat the employer with solidarity.

Second, competitive unionism tends to move the decision making in a campaign from the grassroots leadership to staff, who assume a larger role, are more numerous in a contested campaign, and generally run it in an organization-specific, pretrained manner rather than emerging organically from bargaining unit leadership.

Third, competitive unionism confuses and lowers the of support from potential allies, especially other unions on campus, students, and other community allies. Active public and private support from these allies, especially full-time faculty, is very important in helping to break down fear and fatalism among contingent faculty.

Fourth, in most situations of competitive unionism, the administration, when it cannot easily and openly push a no-union option, surreptitiously supports the union it prefers to deal with. The years of competitive unionism in higher education in California—through the 1970s and into the 1980s—demonstrated this pattern over and over. Some employers even approached their "union of choice" and invited it to enter a campaign, with secret employer assistance. While this situation usually results in a successful union campaign, it may result in a weaker and less militant union with less member participation since it is partly made up of people who would otherwise have voted "no union."

Fifth, competition can be very costly. The resources used for it could better be used for additional organizing or invested in training contingent activists for leadership. These costs also tend to make many in the rank and file more cynical about the higher levels of all unions involved. This encourages a backward parochialism and localism toward the broader union movement that we can ill afford.

Finally, competitive unionism can leave a bitter taste for the leadership of winning union and for the leadership of losing group. These animosities can persist for years, even fueling decertification campaigns, sectarian opposition to agency shop, and spark individual and group challenges to agency fee determinations and "duty of fair representation" charges. These can constitute a continuing weakening of the organizational effectiveness of the bargaining agent to the detriment of faculty. In addition, long-term grudges can lead to discriminatory treatment of the leading participants when representing them on grievances or in bargaining.

Arguments for Union Competition: On the other hand, arguments favor competitive unionism. First, the principle of exclusive representation has not always served U.S. workers well and is not even the most common system of representation in the industrial world. Under U.S. labor laws, exclusive representation in a single bargaining unit means that once a unit is defined, a single organization is then chosen to represent all the workers in that unit and no other union can legally bargain with the employer for these workers. Having multiple unions represent multiple perspectives can sharpen and raise the level of discussion around employment issues while at the same time not necessarily undermine solidarity if decisions are seen to be made openly and democratically. Much of western Europe has multiple representation.

Second, U.S. labor history gives many examples of competitive unionism that drove labor advances. The founding of the American Federation of Labor (AFL) was as a "dual union" with the Knights of Labor in the 1880s. Later, the growth of the AFL between 1900 and 1920 is hard to imagine without the prod of the radical and more inclusive Industrial Workers of the World (IWW). Likewise, the tremendous growth of the AFL after 1935 is impossible to imagine without the formation and competition from the Congress of Industrial Organizations (CIO). The evolution of the National Education Association (NEA) into a union (actively recruiting working teachers, excluding administrators, acting as a collective bargaining agent, calling strikes), especially after the 1960s, was stimulated almost exclusively by the growth of the American Federation of Teachers (AFT), at its expense. Thus the argument is made that however messy, uncomfortable, and expensive in the short run competitive unionism may be, in the long run when openly tied to principled differences, it has served American workers well by pushing both the political level and the energy of the union movement forward.

Third, competitive unionism can force attention to groups that have been ignored or discriminated against by unions, such as contingent faculty, and can cause leadership of existing unions to make commitments and exercise resources on their behalf that they would not have otherwise. This makes the issues of the previously submerged, invisible, discriminated-against group matters of public discussion, and whoever wins will therefore be a better union than either would have been without the competition. One could draw this conclusion from the struggle to unionize public higher education in California in the 1970s and 1980s, where the state AFT affiliate found itself forced both by principle and by organizational rivalry into arguing for combined contingent/tenure track bargaining units against the NEA affiliates, which only wanted to organize the FTTT faculty. In this case, organizational advantage dovetailed with principled solidarity and resulted in better conditions for the vast majority of contingent faculty in the community colleges (where AFT affiliates became the majority) and the state universities (where the NEA affiliate won).

Finally, competitive unionism actually builds the movement in other ways. For one, it causes more discussion and activity than what would take place otherwise, and it also encourages contingent faculty to look for additional structures to pursue their own specific interests and build the specific contingent faculty movement. Basically, this argument says that competitive unionism helps open the door to additional intermediate structures, such as the Coalition for Contingent Academic Labor (COCAL), nationally and locally, and groups such as California Part-time Faculty Association (CPFA) and the Association of Graduate Employee Unions, all of which function across organizational lines and to pressure broader education unions.

My Own Conclusion: The Inside-Outside Strategy: While both sides make many useful points, neither side makes the correct argument. The decades-long debate over "dual unionism" has been a red herring that has not served the labor movement well. Briefly, the question is not one, two, three, or many unions, but rather, what is the political and class content of those organizations and to what degree do they actually represent mobilized democratic, participatory bases among the workers? The assumption of much of the anti–dual union forces over the history of the American labor movement has been that all divisions will be exploited by the employers, especially in the hostile context of the American political economy and must, therefore, be avoided whenever possible. This can lead us to support centralization at all costs, under the guise of rationalization and one union per industry. (Of course, many of these same forces have put their own opposition to dual unionism on hold when their survival or political convictions seem threatened or they wish to expand outside their traditional jurisdiction.) The number of historical counter-examples that the pro-competitive unionists cite demonstrate that organizational variety and competition do not automatically weaken workers.

On the other hand, it is certainly easy to make long lists of examples of competitive unionism campaigns where one side or the other was clearly, if not openly, a company union, or at least the employer's choice—an attempt by the employer to deprive workers of the most militant and democratic representation possible.

Here again, though, the issue is not multiple unions or union competition, but the content of the struggle. One can even find examples of Teamster locals that formerly functioned as cat's-paws for the employers in the farm workers' struggle that have since been transformed into militant, democratic instruments of workers' struggle. Likewise, one can point to victorious NEA affiliates, that, having gone through the wringer of struggle with the AFT, found themselves transformed and built into unified, democratic, and effective unions.

If the proper perspective on this debate is not for or against competitive unionism but rather for or against democratic, participatory social movement unionism, then the question that must be asked strategically is what actions will best bring this about? Contingent faculty in particular, and workers in general, need structures that will allow them to best exercise the highest degree of solidarity and development of class consciousness. In other words, what organizational structure in a particular situation will best provide the maximum amount of activism and class consciousness in any particular situation? This will usually involve multiple organizational structures but not necessarily competing unions. One of the lessons of competitive unionism is that multiple avenues of discussion and attack on particular problems can stimulate change and growth within unions. In other words, "movement building" as opposed to narrow "institution building" is what is needed. This can mean competitive unionism, but it can also mean non-union bodies such as COCAL, CPFA, contingent caucuses in professional organizations (and unions) and other structures that have not yet been fully explored but are likely to be invented in the context of the struggle.

The principle is therefore not one of unitary mechanical formal solidarity but rather a flexible vision of solidarity that strives to unite all who can be united in practice while isolating those who are fundamentally enemies. This has been termed the "inside-outside" strategy.

Its pursuit represents the highest level of strategic thinking available to us in the contingent faculty movement. The historical precedents for such a strategy range from the dual card-holders of the IWW who also worked in their AFL unions to Trade Union Educational League (TUEL) activists in the 1920s, to women and minority caucuses and other formations within hundreds of unions in the 1960s and since. Perhaps the most striking example of this strategy was represented by the Revolutionary Union Movement and the League of Revolutionary Black Workers, which confronted the United Auto Workers and its local and national leaders in the late 1960s. While the success of that strategy was short-lived, the experience of that work and its impact upon the UAW is an example that has never been fully studied with an eye to its general principles as applicable to submerged and discriminated subgroups of workers. This inside-outside strategy has found a partial reflection even within the official AFL-CIO structure with the recognition of the need for "constituency groups," such as the A. Phillip Randolph Institute (APRI), Latin American Council for Labor Advancement (LACLA), Coalition of Black Trade Unionists (CBTU), Asian Pacific American Labor Alliance (APALA), Pride at Work (PAW), and Coalition of Labor Union Women (CLUW).

In sorting out the many arguments about union organizing competition, the fundamental issue remains choosing the process most likely to create a structure for contingent faculty to express their needs through democratic, participatory, social movement unionism. While many of the factors traditionally cited in the "dual union" debate are valid, none of them alone constitute a proper criterion or principled guide for action. These factors all need to be evaluated in the context of the overarching principle. This means that we must all think deeply about our particular situation rather than just apply recipes from outside. Luckily for us as contingent faculty, this is what we do for a living. Together, we can figure out how to advance our interests through this thicket of choices. The future of higher education depends on how well we do this.

The Politics of Lists

In organizing certain archetypes emerge that can symbolize the core values around which an activity is being conducted and also reveal much of the motives of the people who can be associated with that archetype. So it is with the politics of lists and organizing. A central part of any organizing effort is the construction of lists: of activists, of contacts, of potential contacts, of allies, and of enemies. How one constructs one's lists can be seen as archetypal behavior. Three examples drawn from my recent experience in the Chicago area illustrate the point.

Organizing by Clout: In a beginning attempt to organize contingent faculty in a large, multi-campus college district, one union sought to construct a list that included only the most senior faculty (three semesters or more of teaching) and only those who had taught at least six units for each of those three semesters. This list was constructed from Board of Trustees' documents listing the hiring of part-time faculty each semester, and included names, departments and colleges, and teaching load. This list was most accessible to the existing union of full-time faculty who had the negotiated right to see the full board agenda and documents from every board meeting. This list was then supplemented with names drawn from the information of existing FTTT union chapter chairs and department chairs, who were sometimes the same people. In other words, this list was constructed, in a top-down manner, from outside the contingent sector. This list was used to have FTTT union leaders (who also sit on FTTT hiring committees) and department heads (the contingents' direct bosses and FTTT faculty bargaining members) seek out individual part-timers on campus and present them with authorization cards to be signed in a full-timer's presence. Therefore, the list need not include home phone numbers, e-mail addresses, home addresses, or any of the information that would be necessary to have confidential, safe, noncoercive, and egalitarian contact with a workforce made up of fearful and transient workers. This is organizing via "clout" and implied "muscle." This approach precluded a tracking function to record potential member's attitude and action toward the union and the organizing effort. No effort was made to create an actual organization of contingent faculty before card circulation, much less one that would reach beyond the immediate proposed bargaining unit, which comprised only a minority of the contingents.

The list's composition exposed a number of things about the union's strategic pursuits. The union planned no effort to organize all contingent faculty rather only those who taught "credit" classes, and not those of a roughly equal number who taught non-credit continuing education. By focusing only on the most senior and heaviest load "credit" part-timers, the organizers revealed a priority for organizing the easiest, quickest, and cheapest-to-construct bargaining unit, however small a minority (25%) it might be of the total contingent faculty. The list makers preferred those faculty who not only would be the easiest to organize but also would be the most stable: the most likely to stay organized and pay enough dues to support their organizing and subsequent servicing. In this approach, the union showed its reluctance to actually take on, in practice, the legal barriers that existed and instead preferred to take a small group through the perceived "hole" in the law. This strategy was also cheap—requiring few additional staff or money and using existing structures and contacts. Thereby, ensuring no broader strategy for fundamental change in the workplace with so few workers even being considered. This is preeminently a strategy of outside organizing. This is the strategy of an FTTT majority and a full-time union deciding to organize its contingent colleagues in small enough numbers that they would not upset the political balance within the existing union.

Organizing by Money: By contrast, another union, interested in organizing contingent faculty in the Chicago area at about the same time, pursued a different list archetype at that institution. They first filed a Freedom of Information Act request with the Board of Trustees asking for the names, colleges, and teaching loads of all contingent faculty in credit and non-credit continuing education. This had the value of universalizing the group and the potential bargaining unit but provided only a mailing address at a college. This list was then used in a blind first-class mailing to campus addresses with an enclosed information request (not authorization) card to seek potential activists and build a database of contact information.

This list archetype reveals a set of assumptions about strategy and organizing. First, this is the strategy of an organization that has more money and staff than contacts—it can afford to send out expensive, first-class mass mailings in an attempt to generate internal contacts from the outside. Second, it shows a willingness to keep options open regarding the size and composition of an eventual membership or bargaining unit. This is not surprising, considering that this is an outside union with no existing bargaining unit within this employer's workforce and therefore no existing political-economic relationships to be protected. Anything new is a plus for this union. Third, this strategy reveals a desire, through the use of information cards rather than authorization cards, to attempt to build a core of activists within the sector rather than merely having people outside the unit immediately signing workers up as individual, atomized dues-units appended to an existing union body. This second strategy can be seen as outside-in but with some attempt to be bottom up.

Organizing by Grassroots Action: A third list collection effort was under way, generated by an independent organizing committee born out of contacts developed during an anti-privatization struggle of the previous year and the Campus Equity Week activities of fall 2001. This committee consisted of contingent faculty, aided by a few close allies among full-timers, organized clericals, and teachers in the one already organized sector of contingent faculty (the non-credit adult educators teaching who were in yet a third union). Developed piecemeal through the gradual recruitment of a network of activists on all seven campuses, the list focused not on all the members in a potential new bargaining unit but on those who may openly support organizing or who may become active. This list grew to between 5 and 15 percent of the total unorganized contingent faculty and included information such as personal e-mail, home address, phone numbers, and work information such as college, department, and schedule. This list was accumulated from sign-up sheets at meetings, personal referrals from individuals, responses to group e-mails, and campus visits. It existed in a database that also included for each person history of participation and degree of activity, when he or she got involved, and other history relevant to membership in the broader organizing committee. These activists were then asked to create larger lists of their own college or department from their personal contacts and access.

This list archetype demonstrates the importance of building an organizing committee, based on networking with existing activists who would be actual members of the unit. This is an inside-out and a bottom-up strategy. This list also implies that, at this stage of organizing, deep information about individuals who can be involved is more important than aggregate information about large groups who may or may not be reachable in the short term and who may be fairly unstable as contingent workers. This low-cost and low level organizing approach neither relies on existing power structures nor on the expenditures of large amounts of funds or staff.

Finally, this list implies a future organizing strategy keyed on building from existing grassroots political strength to areas of potential grassroots political strength. Authorization cards are not the key goal but a benchmark on the way to building an effective union. This third approach also values protecting the confidentiality of contacts and potential contacts, through initial safe and private interactions.

How a union or group elects to construct bargaining unit lists reveals not only the priorities of the organizers but also reveals the kind of organization it visualizes producing in the end. As every experienced organizer knows, how people are organized initially places a firm stamp on the kind of organization that results. Naturally, all organizing entails some degree of mixture of different orientations, as do the simplified examples given here. However, if we want to end up with high-participation, democratic organizations among contingent faculty, we had better pay attention to those values in our initial organizing.

To wrap up my story, the third group ended up feeling forced to affiliate with group #2 before completing its initial organizing plan. This was largely because group #1 forced a representation election by filing authorization cards with the labor board for an election for the small unit they targeted. Thus, this forced both group #3 to go into election campaign mode long before they wanted to and before they had built the organization they envisioned. The only way they felt they could compete in an immediate card campaign and election was to affiliate with one of the existing unions and gain their resources, and they chose group #2. They then won the subsequent election by a convincing margin and have since bargained a first contract, expanded the bargaining group to include all credit adjuncts after their first semester, and negotiated their second contract in 2005.

Appointment to Union Staff: Promotion or Demotion and for Whom?

Virtually all successful organizing efforts eventually include some role for paid union staff. Since 1995 there has been a major push to allocate more union resources to organizing. This was when the New Voice grouping, led by John Sweeney, won the first contested AFL-CIO leadership election since 1955. Their key proposals for change were increased emphasis and resources on organizing and a generally more member-mobilizing unionism.

While they have been unable to stop the decline of membership, the period since 1995 has seen a revitalization of activity within some unions and among some union allies.

One of their key arguments has been the need to hire staff organizers. Before 1995, most unions were governed by the informal 3 percent rule, in which 3 percent of resources were allocated to organizing. If there were individuals designated as "organizers," that title was frequently combined with other titles; often organizers were existing staff who were being "pushed aside" into an area where they could do no harm, would not cause problems for the elected leadership, and weren't expected to do much good or much of anything. This exemplified the decline of organizing and the shrinkage of unions both in density (percentage of the workforce) and in absolute numbers after the great upsurge of membership in the 1930s and 1940s.

Since the 1950s the hiring of staff for organizing or servicing out of the bargaining units was seen as an individual promotion. Put more bluntly, working for the union was a better and easier job, even if not more highly paid, than working "on the job." This situation, combined with the ultra-legalism of U.S. labor relations practices, especially since the anti-labor Taft-Hartley Act, and the need to bargain over many more social welfare concerns compared to other industrial nations, resulted in a larger percentage of the labor movement being composed of paid staffers, either elected or hired, than in other countries. These paid staffers have tended to develop an extreme (and understandable) aversion to losing their position and going back "to the job." The number of these folks and their motivation to hold on to their positions has deeply marked the American labor movement in the years since the Second World War.

Faculty organizations have not followed this general pattern, for a couple of critical reasons. First, faculty unionism has been growing, unlike the rest of the union movement, so the attitude toward organizing has been different. Second, taking a staff job, either as hired staff or an elected position with partial or full release time, does not constitute a "better job" than being a professor or other professional job. In fact, it was almost universally acknowledged that working for the union was harder work, more stressful, and often, in the early days, paid less. It was also a black mark on your resumé if you decided to go back into professional work since most employers avoid hiring professional agitators.

This situation has been healthy for unions made up of full-time permanent professionals: nurses, teachers, engineers, social workers, and others. The few who do pursue union staff work as career enhancement do so with a deep commitment to the union. This ideological commitment is almost always the primary motivation for professional workers to either run for office or seek union staff positions. Thus, careerism, while certainly not absent, is less in professional unions than in unions in which losing a staff position might mean going back to a "worse" job.

As a result, many elected officers, even with substantial release time, tend not to stay in union positions but return to the job after a number of years, even in the absence of term limits in the union's constitution and by-laws. The exceptions to this pattern are some major local unions and state and national-level organizations, where the pay and prestige of leadership clearly dwarf faculty status. But this represents a small percentage of those who are cashing a check for doing union work. In most faculty unions, the typical "staffer" is part-release time volunteer or elected person who spends something less than half their work time performing union tasks. Even the majority of local union presidents of faculty unions fall into this category. This pattern has been healthy for participation and union democracy, but it has had disadvantages. For one thing, the relative unattractiveness of union work means that relatively fewer people run for office; many faculty unions go decades without a contested election for anything. It is hard to see this as healthy for union democracy and participation. Even if one factors in the famous faculty aversion to direct conflict over important matters, one is left with the feeling that when union leadership is linked with personal sacrifice, rather than perks of office, participation at some leadership levels can decline over time.

Clearly, one alternative—individualist careerism, bitterly contested elections based on personalities rather than program, extensive patronage networks, and other perks—is less attractive than what we find in most full-time faculty unions.

With the growth of contingent faculty, now a majority of faculty members and thereby potentially a majority of the faculty union movement, the dynamic of staff and leadership change in a number of ways, all of which are relevant to organizing strategy. First, if unions organize contingent faculty, the existing faculty unions will need transformation, both in structure and thinking, and in leadership. This is both a potentially dialectical and extremely painful process. In this, faculty unionism parallels the rest of the labor movement, though the pressures to change are less intense, perhaps since the major faculty unions, AFT and NEA, and American Association of University Professors (AAUP) are still growing, unlike most unions.

Second, most contingent faculty have a different attitude about holding union office or staff positions than the attitudes of FTTTs. Holding office and gaining the label of activist or agitator can preclude further employment or advancement to FTTT positions. They could even lose their jobs by "failure to be rehired." However, union staff work is in some ways a better job than being a contingent academic. Quite a number of faculty unions have ended up with ex-contingent activists as their hired staffers. This has created an interesting political dynamic in some faculty unions whereby the sympathy for and understanding of contingent faculty is greater among hired staff than it is among the elected leaders (generally all FTTT) who fear political backlash against them by their FTTT base for appearing to be too sympathetic or favorable to contingent faculty. This attitude represents both a fear of diluting the representation and servicing of FTTT faculty and an elitist prejudice against the workers occupying the "lower tier" of the faculty workforce.

A number of organizing questions arise. How prominent a role should outside staff (meaning outside the potential bargaining unit) play in making the decisions involved in organizing, such as timing, selection of targets, and other tactical decisions? If staff are to be hired internally, on what basis should that hiring be done—full-time or part-time, temporary or permanent, selected by whom, assigned to what duties, part of a staff union bargaining unit.? Should hired staff be paid more than the $30,000 a year, the maximum that most contingent faculty can hope to make? If they should be paid more, how much more? If less, how much less? And what other compensation, as well as how much job security, should go along with these positions? How should these positions compare with the generally more stable, better paid, often unionized, servicing reps in unions?

For low-paid contingents, the existence of even temporary and part-time union staff jobs quickly becomes a major political and economic factor in the dynamic of the organizing campaign. This is a situation that faculty unions have yet to consider strategically, a question that seldom surfaced while organizing tenured and full-time tenure track faculty only.

The most useful answers to these questions will come only through the internal transformation of policies and practices of existing unions and the creation of new organizations. These questions regarding paid staff and union structure are one of the best examples of the need for an inside-outside strategy. The way to solve this seemingly intractable problem is not to make it the main problem but to focus on building a democratic decision-making process. Thereby a situation is created, as so often happens in successful social movements, where how a particular problem is resolved becomes less important because the movement and its "process" propels forward and creates a protective shield from the worst possible consequences of a bad decision. How the question is decided can often become more important than the decision reached.

Another factor to consider is co-optation, or "forgetting which side you are on." Even though union activism at this stage does not usually make us more attractive for employment by higher education administrators, the exceptions are important for the movement. There are cases in which employers have picked out leading activists, organizers, stewards, lower-level elected officers, and local presidents and offered them administrative jobs. Given the insecurity and weaker economic position of contingent faculty, it can only be expected that this will occur more in the future. I have seen it, in a Chicago example, as early as the first contract period where a new, energetic but careerist steward was recruited to be an administrative "liaison" with the union and adjunct faculty (ironically, on a part-time temporary basis). A small crumb, but it was effective, at least until the person got a full-time job elsewhere. The most important factor for our consideration here, however, is not what these people do once they are extracted from the struggle and placed in positions beholden to the employer, but rather what the impact is on the movement. Every organizing effort has a moment in its history when the loss of two or three key leaders can set it back months or even years. As the movement grows, it is to be expected that employers will learn this lesson more thoroughly.

The co-optation is not limited to the employer. Higher union bodies can also affect the trajectory of an organizing effort by their choice of hiring people on staff. This problem extends into the ongoing work of existing faculty unions if they embark on new organizing efforts, increase or change staff, and advertise to hire people. In many cases, the only internal applicants they will receive are contingent faculty, and then they are faced with the decision of whether to hire their own contingent faculty or an outsider. This is not a choice that most full-time faculty union leaders relish.

The general issue is not whether unions should hire contingent activists as staff or if activists should take the jobs. The real issue is the question of power. Who has the power to decide whether hiring is to be done, exactly who is hired and potentially fired, and on what basis? Who has the power to define what the job is, and who do they answer to? These are the questions worth asking in this situation, and the answers provide signposts on the path to movement building, not just bargaining-unit growth. The grassroots movement should be the source of the power to make, or heavily influence, the decisions about staffing, as well as other essential decisions crucial to any organizing effort. This is another example of the need to be close enough to the movement-building end of the spectrum and of the need to pursue a social movement unionism.

The primary question is always this: Are practices being pursued that will build, rebuild, and continually reinvigorate the movement at the base, from which the power, militancy, collectivity, and ultimately political correctives for erroneous decisions flow? For example, suppose a national union is working to organize a group of contingent faculty and chooses to provide resources and support in the form of taking one of their activists and putting him or her on part-time staff at a monthly salary of $1,000. In this case the decision of how to allocate that resource is now made once and for all, and by the national union staff, as long as the person keeps that job. By contrast, if that same $1,000 is allocated to the organizing committee as a grant, and the organizing committee then has to decide whether to use some of it for a newsletter or website, some for a listserv, some to pay gas and an hourly stipend to send one of their members to leaflet or stuff mailboxes on various campuses, then the group both preserves the power to make these decisions and has numerous, repeated opportunities to practice choosing and evaluating how to support and budget its own existing strengths, with support from the larger union. In this instance, "union learning," or real labor education has now occurred and can be applied to future situations as needed.[5] If the committee itself had begun to collect small dues and had some independent money to use for its own choices, it would be even better.

Reverse Engineering a Good Union: Participant Action Research (PAR)

A useful organizing strategy is to perform the intellectual exercise of reverse engineering. Look at a union that functions well. It serves its members honestly, efficiently, and militantly in its day-to-day relations with the employer. It democratically involves the greatest number possible in both the day-to-day functioning of the union and in the tactical and strategic decision making of the union. It consciously pays attention to the continuing need to struggle for solidarity and equality, and thus against inequities in its ranks. It provides a healthy and friendly context in which larger questions of solidarity with other unions and workers throughout the nation and world can be discussed and acted upon appropriately. If this is a reasonable definition of "good" union, then the exercise of reverse engineering can help us take the pieces of that good union apart both functionally and historically and perhaps help us answer the question: How do we build such a union?

Organizers have noted that how a union is first organized, what its principles are, and even what leadership it chooses determines its future functioning. A recent study has reaffirmed that conclusion.[6] I have drawn much of this chapter on strategic considerations from reverse engineering that my colleagues and I have performed over and over again, consciously and unconsciously.

To illustrate how reverse engineering works microcosmically, I will choose one characteristic to examine, both as an example of the exercise and because it is so frequently overlooked.

Participant action research (PAR) serves a good example of a characteristic of a "good union" to examine. In PAR, participants in an organizational or social struggle work as co-researchers in seeking collective social change. It does not mean that all are equal—there is usually a lead researcher—but all are participants in the process. For full participant action research to exist, the project must be collectivized to include secondary participants to help with decisions. This democratic, applied social research is designed to advance a social agenda.

Good unions almost always engage in the constant process of using their officers, executive board members, stewards, and sometimes members in an informal process of participant action research. The best unions combine this constant data gathering with periodic, internally transparent semi-strategic planning so that ideas can flow into planning recommendations for the organization. Perhaps because most unions have remained so closed to outsiders, PAR theory has not really been explicitly applied to unions.

Consciousness of PAR should inform the strategic development of an organizing effort. The hundreds of contract surveys and one-on-one campaigns conducted by stewards and worksite representatives, the day-to-day work of mobilizing, informing, and asking questions of members that take place almost as second nature in a good union, are actually networks of participant action research. Theorizing this process can bring the practice of good trade unionism and its explicit prejudice toward participatory democracy together with the knowledge-creation theory that has been usefully developed in the PAR literature. This would be reverse engineering at its best.

An example of such union-related research occurred during the planning of Campus Equity Week (CEW) 2001 in Chicago. The CEW coalition made a brief survey seeking information on faculty pay and institutional income to compare and to use for publicity and internal education. These were the percentage of regular FTTT pay that contingents earned for the same work—the pro rata percentage or the inequity ratio—and the percentage of institutional per-class income (tuition, state aid) that ended up in contingent instructors' pockets— the rate of exploitation. To do this, the coalition, having no full-time staff, much less a staff researcher, relied on activists to gather this information from their respective institutions. A span of pro-rata percentages at Chicago-area institutions and a span of rates of exploitation were then included in the publicity materials. This is an example of participant action research because the question was posed out of the needs of the struggle and was answered collectively by those who were participating in the struggle. The information was interpreted and analyzed for use both centrally and by participants. And finally, this information was used, in the form of various educational materials, by the whole range of activists involved in the Chicago Campus Equity Week project.

Guide for a National Strategy

1. A national strategy must focus primarily but not exclusively on movement-building, not solely organizational growth. This is properly reflective of the stage we are in now when movement-building should be primary.

2. A national strategy must consider the fear and fatalism resulting from lack of job security and lesser economic power compared with FTTTs as a factor in contingent faculty consciousness and behavior.

3. A national strategy must recognize that the "new majority" faculty are now part of the working class and that their concerns include both economic and job security equity as well as the desire to defend and improve education for their largely working-class students.

4. A national strategy must understand that contingent faculty are part of a casualized workforce and must be organized as a whole workforce on the job and in the community. Further, doing this can play a particularly important role in opening the door to essential coalitions on and off campus.

5. The organizational forms that the movement creates must be varied, fluid, and not necessarily reflective of present trade union structures.

6. A national strategy must be democratic in form, content, and activity, as participatory as possible, and with a leadership that reflects the base in all aspects.

7. A national strategy must be "inside-outside," recognizing the need for independent organization, in whatever form, of contingent faculty, as well as the need for solidarity with FTTT, reflected in as high a level of organizational unity as possible.

3

The Chicago Experience

The following interviews with contingent faculty organizers in the Chicago area provides detailed descriptions of what they learned in order to help others consider options in their own campaigns.

Chicago was a relative latecomer to the organization of contingent faculty compared to both the Northeast and West Coast, where activity extends back to at least the 1970s. The only Chicago area example I could unearth before the passage of the Illinois Educational Labor Relations Act (IELRA, 115 ILCS) in 1983 (effective January 1, 1984) was in the Chicago city colleges among adult educators. This was not specifically union organizing activity, which came about after the law was passed. A fair number of FTTT bargaining units had already been established and gained contracts before this enabling legislation was passed. These cases, most prominently AFT units in the Chicago city colleges and the Board of Governors state university system (not University of Illinois), had come about through direct action, including some hard-fought strikes. None of these units originally included the contingents. I have not been able to ascertain exactly what percentage of the teaching force was contingent in the Chicago area at this time, but the rise in contingent faculty likely took place later in this region than in other sections of the nation.

Map of the Metro Chicago Workforce

On the national spectrum of metropolitan contingent faculty workforces, the public-private mix of metro Chicago's employing institutions falls somewhere near the middle; it is neither overwhelmingly public sector, as in California, nor majority private as in the Boston area.

Metro Chicago has seventy-two large and small private non-profit institutions that employ large numbers of contingent faculty (Roosevelt, Columbia, Northwestern, Loyola, DePaul, National Louis, University of Chicago, and many

Chicago Area Institutions of Higher Education

Type of Institution	No. in the City	No. in the Suburbs
Private		
Non-profit	39	33
For profit	14	12
Public		
University	3	2
Community College	7	13

Source: Illinois Board of Higher Education, http://www.ibhe.org, 2002

lesser-known institutions). Their total number of institutions has declined recently with mergers, and further mergers may be consummated.

The city also has a large public university sector: this includes the University of Illinois, Chicago and Northeastern Illinois and Chicago State Universities. Outside the city there are Governor's State and Northern Illinois. There are twenty community colleges in the greater metropolitan area.

Chicago is a national center of the for-profit higher education industry, with one of its major players, DeVry Institute and University, centered here. It was recently joined by University of Phoenix, offering both graduate and under-graduate degrees in selected fields. This sector includes numerous proprietary trade schools in various fields offering both accredited degrees and trade certifi-cates. Twenty-six are listed as registered with the Illinois Board of Higher Education. There are in-house "corporate universities," such as at Motorola. There are out-of-state-based institutions that offer classes in the Chicago area and employ local contingent faculty.

Finally, although diffuse, there is the large adult education infrastructure divided into two major sectors, with English as a Second Language classes as its largest component. One sector is made up of tuition-free classes, such as those offered by the City Colleges of Chicago's Adult Learning Skills Programs (ALSP), offering programs in English as a Second Language (ESL), high school equivalency test prep (GED), and adult basic education (ABE).

Community groups and churches offer some free classes, but this sector is rapidly shrinking as tax and charitable support for it is declining. The other adult education sector is tuition-based and includes Berlitz language schools, distance education companies, test prep firms such as Kaplan, a private ESL industry, corporate education, unaccredited trade schools, and small group informal teaching and consulting that fades into executive private tutoring and lessons at the high end.

Head Counts: No one has ever taken a complete census of contingent faculty in the Chicago area. I could find no counts at all for the for-profit groups, but indications are that this group is large. This suggestion is supported by extrapolation from estimates made by Perry Robinson of AFT in 1999.1 He estimated that the for-profit sector nationally, in total faculty, might be as large as the entire traditional private nonprofit and public sectors combined (at least 250,000 full-time and 500,000 part-time). Contingent faculty statistics that do exist, for the for-profit and the traditional segments, are usually based on administrative reports, which are uniformly low. The lack of centralized statistical data is partly a function of the decentralization of the hiring and management of these faculty. This situation suggests that the workers' organization or union may turn out to be the force that not only organizes the workers but also "organizes (regularizes) the industry."

Because of the lack of previous studies, the number of contingent faculty in the Chicago area must be inferred from several sources, including reports by the U.S. Department of Education, National Center for Education Statistics, and Illinois Board of Higher Education (IBHE). My best estimates, based on IBHE data for the entire state of Illinois in the public and private institutions and reflecting reasonable assumptions, are at least 16,000 contingent faculty working in the Chicago area. This includes nearly 14,000 part-timers (about 2,000 in public universities, 7,400 in public community colleges, and 4,400 in private institutions). Added to this are the full-time non-tenure track faculty, who total 2,200. These numbers are conservative for the following reasons:

1. The total figure does not include people teaching who are not considered faculty by their institutions, such as graduate employees. This group could easily add 1,000 to 2,000 to the total given the number of Ph.D. and M.A. granting institutions in the area that use graduate employees to teach. They are all contingent.

2. This figure grossly undercounts the formal and informal for-profit sector, being limited to those degree-granting institutions that report to the IBHE. Virtually none of the faculty, full- or part-time, in the for-profit sector have tenure and are therefore at-will employees, with much more similarity to contingents in the traditional institutions than to FTTT faculty. Also, the percentage of these faculty who are part-time tends to increase, in my personal experience, as one descends down the scale of non-degree granting institutions and the increasing informality of employment relationships. I estimate that the true figure here could well add 10,000 to the total, though of course some have multiple jobs in teaching.

3. This figure also leaves out the non-credit classes taught through many of these same institutions. In the Chicago City Colleges alone, this is at least 1,800 adult and continuing education faculty. Again, some of these teachers also teach in one or more places for credit, but I estimate that this group could easily add 5,000 to the total.

4. This figure also leaves out branches in metro Chicago of out-of-state institutions that offer instruction here and often employ contingent faculty here. This number could easily reach the hundreds, but it is basically a guess except to say that it is totally omitted.

The general pattern of undercounting seems to be similar in other states.

My estimate is that there could be 30,000 contingent faculty in the Chicago area. Given multiple jobs, rapid transition in changing employers, and the overall fluidity of this labor force, a solid figure will not be obtained until organizing brings stability to a major portion of the workforce. At that time, if the experience in California is any indication, then the hyperactive motion of this sector may have slowed enough to count contingents. By then it can be reasonably predicted that there will be fewer contingents to count because a higher percentage of them will be working more classes, with fewer employers, at something approaching a living wage, and therefore with less turnover.

Demography: The composition of the sector has similar experience in other parts of the country. Women are disproportionately represented, especially in ESL, humanities, and composition.[2] Based on interview data, personal experience, and observation, there may be a higher proportion of black contingent faculty in Chicago than in many other areas. This is because historic centers of black educa-

Table 2: Illinois Demographic Public Sector Faculty Profile

DEMOGRAPHIC CHARACTERISTICS	Public Universities			Community Colleges	
	FTTT	FTNTT	PTNTT	FTTT	PTNTT
Female	32.2%	51.0%	44.8%	39.3%	46.2%
Male	67.8%	49.0%	55.2%	60.7%	53.8%
Median age	50	47	45	50	47
ETHNICITY					
White	82.3%	83.8%	82.5%	83.1%	79.9%
Black	5.6%	4.9%	7.9%	8.1%	9.9%
Hispanic	2.5%	3.0%	2.4%	1.0%	2.3%
Asian-American	8.3%	6.1%	5.0%	6.7%	4.6%

tion are here (Roosevelt, Chicago State, certain of the community colleges, Northern Illinois in some fields, Governor's State), and because Chicago is still one of the most segregated cities in America and alternative employment opportunities for educated black people remain severely constricted. The statistical research to support these speculations remains to be done. However, these factors retain importance in constructing an organizing strategy.

Another demographic fact with implications for organizing is that, as a capital of the Midwest region, Chicago draws many people from the surrounding states for employment. While few come to Chicago to work as adjunct faculty, many may have gone to college in Chicago, accompanied spouses, or taken jobs they no longer have, and hence find themselves in this labor force with limited freedom to leave, which is characteristic of many of the metropolitan areas.

Income: Because of the relatively low pay (as low as $1,200 for a three-unit, fifteen-week course and probably averaging well under $2,000), virtually all part-timers have more than one job or source of income. In addition to those who teach in more than one place, some have multiple jobs teaching or are doing other work for the same institutions. These can include teaching and counseling, teaching and tutoring, teaching and community outreach, teaching and clerical or technical work, teaching and any one of a number of academic professional jobs. Some are public school teachers compensating for the decline in their salaries. Some have other full-time or part-time jobs outside academia, ranging from curators of art galleries to low-level clerical, hospitality, and taxicab work and including various forms of "consulting." Some have two or three "businesses" as supplementary self-employment. There is also a relatively small group of independent professionals and business people—real estate brokers, physicians, lawyers, and others who more closely approximate the pre-1970s contingent faculty as community professionals to share their expertise and for whom the direct compensation is of little importance. There are also people temporarily teaching part-time who may have had full-time jobs before but because of family obligations, health problems, or other difficulties, can now only work part-time or cannot make a long-term commitment to a particular employer. Retirees are yet another segment, either retired from college teaching, K-12 teaching, or from other work. A final category includes those who make up the rest of their living from unearned income, either income of their spouse, inherited wealth, investments, or rents. Individual faculty may fall into more than one category at a time.

To my knowledge no comprehensive studies that could reliably quantify these employment and income categories exist. The following table is from IBHE and covers the public sector for the entire state. Chicago figures are perhaps somewhat higher. These figures are useful because they are adjusted for percentage of a full-time load the average part-timer is carrying (full-time equivalent, FTE). Here we see the great distance from equity or "equal pay for equal work" that currently exists. Research conducted by the Chicago Coalition for Campus Equity Week showed pro-rata figures lower than 50 percent in all cases, including the private sector, with the exception of FTNTT faculty.

For example, the $16,200 in the bottom row under PTNTT meant that a half of all non-tenure track part-timers in public universities, if they worked the equivalent of a full-time load at their present rate, would only make $16,200 per year. This is compared to slightly less for their part-time colleagues in the community colleges at $14,200. It is radically less than what the full-time tenured

Table 3: Annual Illinois Public Sector Faculty Pay, Fall 2000

	Public Universities			Community Colleges	
SALARY	FTTT	FTNTT	PTNTT	FTTT	PTNTT
Mean Salary	$66,000	$42,800	$13,000	$53,800	$6,200
Median Salary	$50,400	$30,400	$8,000	$49,800	$4,000
Full-time Equivalent					
Mean Salary	$66,600	$42,800	$34,400	$53,800	$15,000
Median Salary	$62,200	$30,400	$16,200	$49,800	$14,200

Source: IBHE *All Faculty Matter!* 2002

and tenure track faculty in public universities earn, half of whom make more than $62,000 for the same work.

The additional income question is key for organizing for at least two reasons. First, it is a major propaganda point made by those who oppose improvement in conditions for contingent faculty. Administrators have argued for decades that contingent faculty do not work primarily for money and thus do not need, or want in many cases, the traditional perquisites, compensation, or responsibilities of faculty. Answering this propaganda is crucial in any successful organizing strategy. Second, the diversity of economic situations that actually exist among contingent faculty gives rise to a diversity of motivations, consciousness, and perspectives. This is not a unique problem in this sector: the organization of factory workers in the early part of the twentieth century required confronting a similar variety of origins and personal situations, although perhaps not as extreme. These considerations should push organizers toward those demands that can unite this group, even though these faculty will not all place the same priority on all demands that they support. Also, pursuing unifying demands can help raise contingent faculty consciousness about their actual place in the class system—that of highly exploited professional intellectual workers.

Unionization: Illinois is not one of the top ten states for unionization of higher education faculty; there were only 7,762 organized faculty in 2002, most of whom were in FTTT-only bargaining units.[3] Nearly all organization is in the public sector, with the exception of the two new IEA adjunct units at Roosevelt and Columbia in Chicago, which together total between 1,000 and 1,500. Columbia is one of only four contingent bargaining units that cover the majority of the possible faculty, in its case probably over 90 percent. The others are the adult educators at City Colleges of Chicago, with over 800 members represented by AFSCME 3506. Roosevelt's unit now includes nearly all adjuncts after their first semester. All of the other represented groups are relatively small, under 200. Elgin (IFT), Oakton (IEA), and College of DuPage (IEA) are all currently units of between 100 and 150; in each case the number represents a minority of contingent faculty. Northern Illinois's IFT unit represents about 120 FTNTT, but leaves out the majority of other contingents. The IFT units in the former Board of Governors' schools likewise represent minority fractions and all are under 100 in what they call their B-units.

The total unionization in metro Chicago for contingent faculty is about 2,650, and even if we allow for members who are not teaching in a current semester, 3,000 would be a generous estimate. Of these, about 550–600 are in IFT/AFT locals, 800 in AFSCME, and the remainder in IEA/NEA locals. All units have agency shop, and in all cases the vast majority are members rather than agency fee payers.[4] (People who choose not to actually join the union must, if provided in the contract, pay a "fair share" fee equal to the cost of representing them in negotiations and grievances, about 80 to 95% of regular dues.) Taking my high of 30,000 and minimum of 16,021 estimates of total faculty in the Chicago area, the most generous 2,650 estimate of unionized contingent faculty yields a unionization rate of between 10 and 19. This is higher than nearly any other contingent workers except the building trades, but well below the figure for FTTT faculty or for the public sector workforce generally. It is well below the level needed to exercise leverage on employers and government for improvement. The fact that no Chicago area representation election among part-time contingents has ever been lost (and only one nationally) demonstrates that these numbers could increase more rapidly than is common in the labor movement.[5]

Organizers' Voices

These are voices from virtually all of the organizing efforts up to 2002 in the Chicago area. The names of the various organizers quoted below have been changed to protect their identity, with the exception of Tom Suhrbur and Earl Silbar, who specifically asked to be named properly. I myself was involved at Roosevelt, the second Columbia campaign, and less so at the American Academy of Art and College of DuPage.

How and Why We Got Involved: Many organizers have a history of social activism in the antiwar movement, civil rights movement, or previous union organizing. Whatever the focus, they always see themselves as activists. Earl Silbar, an organizer of adult educators at the Chicago city colleges, explained:

> The civil rights movement, the antiwar movement and socialist and communist ideas, and the experience that there is a ruling class, that we live in a class-dominated society, and that I have experienced and been in struggles where we forced people in power to do what they did not want to do—from forcing university administrations to being part of a global movement with successful revolutionary movements—it runs in my blood.

Silbar made this link between his history as an activist and the commitment to organizing among adult educators:

> When I was working in a machine shop and we had a union, I was active with a number of coworkers to try to change the conditions, because I believed in that possibility, not because I read about it, because I experienced it and I read about what explained it. So when there was an organizing drive, it was like, of course, this is what we should do. We would be fools if we didn't do it.

Tim Cook, of Columbia College, also had an activist history. He had been a member of the Milwaukee school integration committee, had done "political stuff of one sort or another," been involved in the antiwar movement, and wrote his dissertation at the University of Chicago on the history of police in New York. He finished his dissertation in 1995. "I knew [organizer] Steve Jacobs and may have signed a couple of circulars. I may have started going to meetings in '95," he said. By then he was teaching the history of Chicago and labor history. He felt, with the dissertation finished, "I ought to do something with social utility if I did not have a job beyond Columbia."

Personal feelings of being exploited and discriminated against are a common motivation. Ruth Voss, an elected leader of the part-timer association at

College of DuPage, told the story of how this perspective grew out of her experience. "I applied for positions but never got them. 1988, 1990, 1994 ... and it came down to myself and a person with a Ph.D., and they hired her. Then she taught for a year and went into administration. In 1998 the college opened up another search. It went to another person from another school." Ruth explained that she was rejected for that position because she did not have current or recent credit hours. The reason for this was because she was teaching at College of DuPage, working in a restaurant to make extra money, and teaching in two other schools. Finally, "I got involved actively in CODAA because of my colleagues who said I helped them when they needed the help. I told them, 'Don't think this will do you any good.'"

Some organizers expressed surprise that after years of acting on "other people's issues" that there was a struggle to be fought right where they were and that they could bring their past experience and skills to bear on it. Olive Light, of Roosevelt, tells how personal circumstances and the realization that she was being exploited coincided with her commitment to participating in the organizing drive:

> I know for myself I felt like it was a great opportunity to teach, get something on my CV, and I was very excited. And now I look back and think, "Yo! You are a labor historian. Isn't this a little exploitative?" Then after first semester we bought a house and my salary was mortgage money. It started to feel a lot different and that sort of coincided with the organizing drive. It fit for myself personally. We were looking for a house just as I got involved.

A perceived change in the conditions—feeling like "family" to feelings of exploitation—also triggers activism. Other organizing research indicates that perceived change in workers' conditions motivates activism more than actual conditions. People are more likely to organize when they believe they must defend what is threatened or has been recently taken away. Changing conditions in higher education would suggest that this motive is likely to become more common. Karl Black, leading full-timer but at-will employee organizer at American Academy of Art, tells this story of how his view of unions changed:

> I had never liked unions. I always felt that unions basically held you back. I worked in Western Electric. They started to organize while I was there. I was threatened that if I did not support the union, my tires would be slashed. I was threatened personally by a union organizer. Physical threats, and I did

not join. I had to pay dues even if I was not a member. I was totally, absolutely against unions my entire life. I changed when this owner took over. My very eye opened as to how a private individual could mess up a lot of people's lives. So now I am for unions.

Kathy Moon, FTTT activist at Governor's State, was comfortable with organizing because of her father's experience with the post office:

My father belonged to the union at the Post Office and was not active, but the union saved his job 3 times. [He] never got along with bosses and managed to get fired several times and the union always got his job back so I always felt indebted to the union. I never thought about it much because I thought professionals don't need unions.... I first found out GSU was unionized at my interview. I had just gotten hurt by not having protection [on a former job] so it seemed a useful way to go. I am a pragmatist. I had no intention of becoming active in the union. I did not become an officer until I was tenured, but I did picket. I probably would have [been more active] if someone had asked me, but nobody did.

For others, it is as simple as being asked by an organizer who had set a good example. Deb Brown, part-timer and volunteer organizer in the Oakton campaign, said:

I remember when I was first approached about it, my first concern was, what is to prevent me from getting fired? This goes back fifteen years. No part-timers were doing this. I remember being told there were no guarantees. But I guess over a period of time enough of us decided we were willing to make some kind of a commitment to see where this would go.

When asked, "What made you overcome your fear?" she answered:

I suppose it was the dedication and commitment of the original individuals. Fortunately, my day-to-day existence did not completely depend on working at Oakton. I was not eager to give up the job, but I would have survived. It was just inspiring to see Jim and Karen, that they could make this kind of commitment, then some of the rest of us could come along.

That people conjure such memories over a decade later shows an emotional content and historical importance critical for organizing. It also helps explain why these individuals were successful organizers—they were still in touch with how they got involved. The people who could not remember how they got involved and could not tell a story beyond one line were not people who maintained their activism.

Campaign Beginnings: Sparks and Issues: Long intervals of no pay raises, while watching others getting raises and inflation rising, most commonly sparks organizing campaigns. Flo Smith speaks of Northern Illinois University's 1988 campaign launching after receiving no pay raises for eleven years, "someone sent out a flyer from [the] education [department]. So we would meet in a room, with no management around and cluster around a table with about six to eight education people [and] started comparing notes."

Earl Silbar described a trek to the board of the city colleges:

In winter of '86 I and a few others went down to the board meeting in December and I made a presentation about how it is hard to celebrate Christmas when you are going to be laid off for three weeks without pay. Five years without an increase is what really laid the basis for it.

Deb Brown at Oakton said, "The main issue was pay. We had not gotten a raise in seven years; $300 a credit hour, per semester."

At Columbia, Steve Jacobs described surveying contingents about what they were actually making:

We did a survey of part-timers to see if our understanding was correct about what we were feeling—if we really had people in the same ballpark. Which reassured us a lot, because we did get some hard numbers on people's income—how much they taught, how much they depended on part-time teaching as part of their income. One-third had less than $10,000 [total] income and another third ten to twenty thousand, so that blew [the administration's argument]. The administration liked to talk about Columbia as a professional school and that these are highly paid professionals teaching here part-time.

Karl Black reported that at the American Academy of Art, "our new director said you could be fired for talking about how much money someone is making. So we knew that was a dead end." This also told them that comparing pay would be a key way to organize.

After pay, comes job security, the feeling that job security had become more threatened than before. Olive Light explained:

Working conditions varied tremendously across the board—almost feudal
... People felt very underpaid and lacking long-term stability with the institution. Even for people who had taught for years and years, it could really
be hit or miss whether you got classes or not.

Sally Edwards, from Chicago State, described how a particular administrator's behavior exacerbated the sense of insecurity:

We had a horrible president. Our enrollment was dropping. He would do
things like someone would come in the morning and the locks would be
changed in the office. He was the best recruiting tool we could possibly have
had. The main concern was job security.

A consistent refrain among organizers is their complaint of impossible
teaching conditions and their concern for the content of education and the welfare of faculty members.

Often administrations that refuse to respectfully treat modest collective proposals for change presented by unofficial committees spark the organizing fire.
Steve Jacobs, organizing committee at Columbia College, described a critical
turning point in 1995:

At the end of this period we again met with the administration and they
said, "Well, that's all very nice but there is really nothing we can do about
it." A couple said they used to be part-time teachers. At the end we asked
them, "Okay, if there is one thing, will you form a commission with part-
timers on it to investigate the condition of part-time faculty?" Several weeks
later they sent us a letter saying no. It was not possible to do that. That's
really what sort of set us off. We were getting nowhere this way.

Two organizers spoke of their campaigns being sparked by statements
from national organizations—statements about the importance of organizing
contingent faculty for better treatment. Likewise, some organizers spoke
about how their early lack of knowledge of activity in other places in the
country left them feeling alone, fearful, and hesitant. As time passed, organizers of later campaigns repeatedly referred to learning of successes at other
local campuses. Olive Light: "Tom Suhrbur gave us the scoop about what had
happened at Columbia, and that is what really piqued people's interest at
Roosevelt." The story reached Karl Black at the American Academy of Art as
well: "The other factor that influenced me was the success of Columbia

College. Some of our part-time teachers were working there, too, so we were getting information."

Exploiting existing formal or informal gatherings of part-timers, whether called by the administration, or accidentally created by the existence of gang offices pushed many campaigns forward. Earl Silbar:

> City Colleges used to have, in '79 and '80, citywide regular meetings where all teachers would come together and have workshops. That was when I got my first impression because there was actually an organizing drive going on. It was a pretty radical group of people. There were activists influenced certainly by the '70s and some the '60s. All of them were community based and their attitude was that this education exists to serve the community, education is a tool for liberation, so it was a pretty feisty group in the late '70s.

Olive Light said that, prior to the first organizing meeting, she "did not know any adjuncts at all. This is the first time I saw who I worked with."

In one case a low-level administrator mobilized other employees to pressure the president around his own personal issues. The other employees severed themselves from him and decided to organize a union. Hal Jones, from Metropolitan, a for-profit, told the following story of the mid-1980s:

> The deputy administrator, who had recruited me, was having some conflict with the president of the campus. Because he had hired a lot of the teachers and staff, he sort of mobilized a protest and we all walked into the president's office. This guy [the deputy administrator], made some play. I forget what the issues were about, but for us, for the staff, the issues were extremely low wages and typical workplace issues. I was making something like $14,000 a year as a teacher. The secretary and receptionist were working full-time and qualified for food stamps. What I did almost immediately was I took a bunch of teachers to have lunch and I said, "Let's cut him [the deputy administrator] loose. He's a loose cannon. He has these personal issues with the president. We should get serious and bring a union in." Everybody said yeah, that sounds great. No resistance to the union idea at all.

The full-time tenure track leaders who decided to organize contingents had to face some opposition from within their own ranks. One of them, Stan Davis at Elgin, said that there were two years of discussion leading up to the vote in March 1990. The vote was,

...to say the least, extremely contentious. The vote was very close, like 33 to 26 or so. ... Later, we had two full-time faculty union members go to testify to the [labor] board that was against our petition. The arguments against included different hiring basis, that we would be overwhelmed by them [numerically]...I think there was also just a fear of change. Fear of the unknown. But, the pie can be bigger. The school could charge more for its services. So they outnumber us, so what? What are they going to do? Kick us out of our offices? It's kind of a ridiculous argument. I don't know what the part-timers would do to us. First and foremost it is a simple justice issue. It's the right thing to do.

Kathy Moon, the full-timer from Governor's State, described how the decision to organize contingents took place:

I was [formerly] a contingent and I know what kind of hell they go through and felt they should have some protection. Some of the [full-time] faculty said you shouldn't have done it without a faculty vote. Only the union executive committee voted. In the senate, there was some objection because some of these people were hired without peer review and now they would be protected by the union and some of them really don't have the credentials. My answer was that what we need to do next is get a good peer review system and we need to be involved in selection of contingent [lecturers], who are not the same as adjuncts, which are not in unit. In the next contract we would like to have peer review on more of the selection of lecturers and evaluation ... not only by deans and chairs. I said these people have been there and they deserve protection.

How We Chose a Union: The most common story about choosing a union is a story of rejection. Deb Brown from Oakton Community College put it simply: "We went with IEA because they were the only ones that would have us." The story of rejection—either overt hostility or explicit lack of interest by full-timer-led faculty unions—is one of the saddest chapters in faculty unionism. Earl Silbar from the Adult Educators at City Colleges remembered their initial organizing effort in 1979–81:

We asked AFT to help us organize. At that time, we weren't covered by the law. And they didn't extend themselves. SEIU did give us some resources and some help. But we did not end up with a union, no. When the law was passed in '85 a few of us who had always been interested in having a union went to the AFT leadership on our campus and asked them for their help because they had the right to information; since they were a recognized union they could get list of all the teachers and all their phone numbers.... They basically blew us off. They said you are mostly people who are just in it for spending money and ring money and you're just part-timers. You're not serious about this and we're not going to bother.

The third effort, the one that finally brought in a union, took place in 1987:

We were interviewing AFSCME, UAW, Teamsters, and SEIU and some people made overtures to AFT. ... AFT doesn't want to come along and they are the natural because we're teachers. We're working for the same colleges, and they are the big union already there. They have already won major breakthroughs. They got one of the best, if not the best, contracts in the country in the community colleges. [Two of our activists] had past experience with SEIU and AFSCME and they knew that AFSCME was very close to management despite its progressive rhetoric on being antiracist, anti-apartheid. ... In the end, the two of them and...myself were the only ones against AFSCME. So we went with AFSCME.

Other factors that played a major role in union affiliation includes the perception of whether this union had a serious progressive history, a perception of previous success in organizing "people like us," or whether the organization "just wanted dollars and bodies and was not prepared to really help us." Hal Jones, a Metropolitan organizer, tells this story:

The main question was what union to bring in. Most of these people did not have union experience, but they had civil rights experience. ...One guy had been in and around the Black Panther Party. Sort of the whole social, civil rights, progressive mentality of the black community was what was really pushing it.... We went and visited PUSH [People United to Save Humanity, led by Jesse Jackson], before going to SEIU, but the first thing PUSH wanted was money. It was really opportunist. We just walked away from them. Then [we] went to SEIU.... I suggested an SEIU local I knew led by this guy who was a really decent progressive great guy, who by himself went out and organized these locals in the '60s, mainly of very poor women in the service industries. My dad, who was involved in the labor movement, knew him.

Even inexperienced committees gave serious consideration about their future. There was, for instance, feeling in favor of being in the same overall organization as the full-time faculty even in cases where the full-time faculty were indifferent or hostile to the part-time organizing. Ruth Voss, leader of the part-time association at College of DuPage, said: "We knew the [FT] Faculty Association was IEA and that might be more efficient to get full-time sympathy." But this concern played both ways. Steve Jacobs from Columbia College's PFACC:

> We started calling unions, AFT and IEA and UAW and a couple others. We chose to go with IEA and the reasons were basically because, with AFT we would have been folded into a large local, and we wanted to run our own show.

Committees also discussed the advantages of being in a "teachers' union" that "might know our concerns better" rather than being in a union such as AFSCME or SEIU that represented workers other than teachers. Tim Cook from Columbia College explained:

> My brother in the AFSCME local [3506 in City Colleges] once said to me, "We're a union with people in hospitals and collecting garbage and what do they know about being a teacher? You really want to think about getting in a teachers' union."

Sometimes the choice was made under forced conditions. Flo Smith from Northern in DeKalb remembered this experience with AFT 4100 in 1991–92:

> We held the meeting at University Hall and there were five or six of us there. And we invited them to talk. They gave us the pitch about joining the union and [how] they would help us get more wages, more rights, and try to rectify some of the problems. But the kicker was that then he says you have the next twenty minutes to decide. They left the room, while the six of us sat there and tried to decide if we wanted to commit to organizing the temporary faculty. We had no real idea who people were. We called them back in and told them we would attempt to do this. ... [Then we were told] we need to have all the cards by March.

What We Did Right: The collective expression of the organizers was that virtually everything that was done was worth doing, or at least not harmful. This supports the research of Kate Bronfenbrenner and others who have quantitatively documented that the more innovative membership-involving tactics used, the more effective the organizing. These tactics build on each other in a geometric fashion, not merely an additive one.

The two activities that organizers said were right fell into two categories: skill-building and group development and the other campaign tactics.

Under the first, they listed such things as learning to make decisions and to act on them collectively and learning to overcome fear, often through the discussion of inspirational or courageous acts by one of their number. Earl Silbar at City Colleges remembered:

> We had to make lots of decisions, like what to do when management challenged our right to pass out our newsletter. ...[One of our activists] was challenged and just continued to pass them out, just ignored the administration. He set an example that was inspirational.

Another skill was learning perseverance, to keep getting lists and continuing to search for people because, when found and contacted, people were overwhelmingly positive. Hal Jones reported on the organizing effort at Metropolitan:

> The secretary of the president was pro-union and would sneak us these documents. They thought we were getting them out of the garbage. We would hit them back every time they hit us. ...Within one week we had 45 or 47 of the [approximately 50] employees on cards. It was that easy. We went for everybody in the whole place.

Along with learning the value of persistance were learning importance of timing and momentum and the awareness of appropriate levels of security and secrecy, especially in the intimidating environment of the for-profit schools. Karl Black explained:

> We felt that because of the owner [of the American Academy of Art] we had to do it under extreme secrecy, so we each contacted one person we felt we could trust. It might seem a little strong to most people but we kind of tried to do it just like the French Resistance in the Second World War. We wanted to time it so management was busy elsewhere and not notice because we knew what Otto [the owner] would do if he found out. We would be gone in a second. We waited to time it during our accreditation inspection. It was not only accreditation but also enrollment [registration] so management gave a lot of attention to that. So we spent that time contacting other people.

For campaign tactics, organizers stressed the importance of being honest in all communications. Deb Brown from Oakton put it emphatically: "[You] have to be honest with people. You get into big trouble if you get into organizing and start promising people all sorts of things and then can't do it."

Another aspect is realizing the value of every direct contact with a contingent faculty member, because they were so difficult to make and sustain, and should be evaluated and strategized about. Tim Cook from PFACC said: "To have any kind of contact is precious, outside of on the phone or by e-mail. These personal contacts are very important and I keep struggling to find out how to have more of them."

Organizers recognized that people will sign cards and support the organization after a direct contact. Such discussions should be conducted in places where they were comfortable and not afraid to talk, in offices with the doors closed, cafes close to campus, or home phone calls. Flo Smith from DeKalb reported:

> Each of us took a list to contact them in person or call them. We did that the entire semester. One reason we were able to do it so quickly was that we were not working against the university because they did not know about it. [We had] lots of phone contact, going into buildings and searching in offices. We planted [the staff organizer from the union] in the McDonald's on Lincoln Highway and asked people to see him if they had any questions. ... Many would not talk to me at work. They would call me at home. There is still a fear factor. A lot of people are very happy to have me doing this because I am the front person.

Reminding contacts that the committee members were faculty too, not outsiders, helped diffuse fear. Steve Jacobs said:

> We would say, PFAC has been around for three years. You know us. We have been teaching here just like you. We are not some outside agitators who are trying to do something secret. It certainly helped us to rebut the outsider charge.

Linking the lack of respect and discrimination for contingent faculty with the educational process and their desire to provide quality education proved a powerful message. When expressed properly, these messages could be extremely liberating and could improve their self-image in a way to allow them to engage in further collective action. Earl Silbar said that this was key to organizing contingent faculty as contrasted with organizing in other workplaces:

Everyone on the organizing committee were people who were deeply committed to the work we did, that is to say working with other adults, mostly working-class people. ... It's different. I have been in other organizing committees. I used to work in machine shops and factories.... It changes the situation when people feel that their job is something special, who take joy in it, get a lot of satisfaction out of it. Some of our people have a missionary attitude.

Yet the bottom line was still money and job security: "I would say the big majority wanted to get more money, wanted to get some security." Organizers learned to incorporate this into the message. Tom Suhrbur, IEA organizer at the American Academy of Art, Columbia, and Roosevelt said: "Part-timers are insulted by their treatment. They are thoughtful and well-educated people and expect better treatment and are not getting it so anything the college does insults them more than anything. Even people who do not need the money to survive are insulted by the pay. You can nurture that in an organizing campaign."

Tim Cook also spoke about contingents' need to be respected as teachers, and the liberating effect of hearing that message spoken by the organizers:

It really is a goal for an awful lot of our members to be better teachers and take care of the students. We insisted that discrimination [against contingents] was a big issue. That [organizing] was the right thing to do. A lot of members feel that that's liberating, adds to the expectations of some people who have not had the feeling of being proletarianized. There are other people who have gotten used to the notion that they are going to be beaten down and they need to think positively about themselves. In a small way there is a kind of psychological liberation that can be involved in thinking this kind of way. I think we did the right thing and we need to keep doing it and keep remembering it.

The form of contact was seen as less important than its frequency and content. Campaigns ranged widely in whether their key communication was one-on-one, face-to-face contact, phone calls, extensive literature, or more recently, e-mail and websites. Faculty, organizers said, can be approached on the basis of extended articles and will read them if they see them as relevant to their lives. Steve Jacobs from Columbia College described their print campaign:

[You] can actually organize through the printed word. We really had to do everything in terms of print organizing. We created a couple of different publications. One was more newsletter format and the other had longer discussion articles. We could only gauge it by the number of cards we were getting. We did mass mailings, cards in mailboxes, personal contact. We got a lot of cards back this way. A lot was not personal contact. People were ready.

He added: "We are an organization that essentially established ourselves with credible literature. We have to assume that our constituency is intelligent and reads." Given that this campaign was at arts-oriented Columbia, print might appear in unexpected places: "We thought of a petition on the sidewalk outside in chalk, and the artists, and get TV cameras."

Most organizers felt the need to send out written surveys to determine membership desires, but those surveys not only construct campaign and bargaining agendas but also confirm the committee members concerns. The collective self-confidence-building function of institution-wide surveys in some cases was more important than the content of the survey, since the organizers were clear on what *they* thought the issues were to begin with.

Several organizers spoke about the need to be politically sensitive and nuanced about the institution by using its own mission statements and image as a service-oriented, educational, and progressive institution as a certain kind of organizational judo to deflate administrative rhetoric. Challenging that image with the reality of pay rates—a mere 7 or 11 percent of the tuition revenue generated—proved effective at Roosevelt University. Olive Light explained how organizers used the legacy of Franklin and Eleanor, for whom the university is named: "All over Roosevelt are quotes from FDR and Eleanor, and we found how to put the thorn in the lion's paw [by using those quotes]. That really worked." Columbia College also had a liberal past. Tim Cook said:

At Columbia we figured it was a liberal institution. Until '92 the president was an old lefty. The current vice president made a speech against the war when he graduated in '68. A lot of people were embarrassed to be on the wrong side of an organizing drive. We always felt we had that going for us and making an issue of that would be to our benefit.

Tom Suhrbur elaborated:

Columbia and Roosevelt both started from a very liberal left tradition. ... A Columbia College founder was well known in liberal left politics, [supporting] low tuition for city kids to get art, music, dance, etc. Roosevelt was founded by a walkout by faculty after WWII at the YMCA college over integration. Faculty formed their own college, and the Y college no longer exists. They adopted Eleanor and Franklin Roosevelt to show their commitment to progressive politics. We used that in each college. Neither college wanted to fight us publicly. We figured we could get an election with minimal resistance and could bargain a decent contract, which we did at both institutions. There was only minimal offensive against our organizing.... Columbia knew they would have to pay a heavy media price if they fought us. To their credit, it worked out very well. At Roosevelt every piece of [our] literature had quotes about the New Deal from FDR on workers' rights. By using that labor FDR tradition we knew the college would have a very difficult time putting on an offense against us.

Political timing had to be part of the strategy. Ruth Voss described how this strategy developed at College of DuPage. The FTTT faculty were coming up for negotiations, expected them to be difficult, and wanted the assurance of the part-timers that part-timers would not cross a picket line should the full-timers go out on strike. Voss was invited to come and speak to the faculty senate, which was also the executive committee of the union. She told them that she personally would not cross a picket line and would ask the members of CODAA, of which she was a leader, to do the same. Several different factors were converging at that time. Campus Equity Week 2001 was just around the corner as were the IBHE (Illinois Board of Higher Education) hearings on HB1720. State Senator Cronin was coming to Du Page for these hearings, which would be attended by over a hundred faculty. Voss said:

> The trustees could see that the timing of bad publicity just before the referendum was bad for them if it went to labor board [for unit hearings on our petition]. The referendum was for a bond issue for the college district, always difficult in anti-tax Du Page County and especially so since the FTTT faculty were singularly unenthusiastic after a very unpopular contract settlement. The district did not need any more bad publicity.

Building alliances with other workers and unions, especially clericals, students, the press, and FTTTs fuels momentum. Steve Jacobs described the outreach at Columbia:

> We put out appeals to students. ... We were able to get a letter from a full-time faculty in support of our drive that we published. We left our newsletters in

full-timer boxes, too. We talked with some AAs in some departments. We felt like we were able to learn for ourselves that there was not a big swell of hostility out there. We found there was a lot of sympathy. There were a lot of students and full-timers who were bitter about this and wanted something to do.

Tom Suhrbur raised the idea of using student newspapers, not only to make students the allies of contingents and to create a public image of the organizing effort, but also simply as a way of communicating with contingents:

> We put ads in student newspapers, part-timers wrote in, it was very important to have good relations with student editors and we felt students were very supportive of us. We wanted as much coverage as possible. Administrators are sensitive to public image. Another reason is that it is hard to get information to part-timers. How do you communicate? Some part-timers don't have boxes or don't check them. We wouldn't get an accurate list until the election.... We never know exactly who is working. So the paper was a way to get information to part-timers themselves.

Olive Light talked about finding allies among the clerical and secretarial workers:

> We knew we needed to do a survey and find out who worked there and we did that by writing down names off mailboxes. But [this] left out scads of people. So we asked secretaries, who in many cases were very, very helpful. Maybe that was from their [experience with their] own [union] organization and their less than perfect contract settlement. Their organization was very friendly and we have tried to reciprocate.

What Did Not Work? The list of what didn't work is much shorter than the list of what did. Most were omissions of actions that organizers wish they had been able to devote more time to. Not a single action taken was mentioned, even under direct probing, as doing more harm than good. If it involved members in activity, then the campaign action can't be bad, no matter what mistakes made in its planning or execution. This result contradicts received wisdom that campaigns must be tightly orchestrated and professionally strategized. This finding suggests that anything that gets more people in motion is good. This may, of course, be specific to contingent faculty or contingent casualized workers in general or it may have much broader application.

Attempting to create large group meetings often proved a fruitless endeavor, especially among part-timers. Many organizers noted that this was the least efficient way to communicate with or draw people into the campaign, despite the urgings of outside organizers, who drew on standard organizing procedure. Still individual contacts were often made at those "unsuccessful" meetings and discussions among the members of the organizing committee in these semisocial circumstances sometimes bore fruit.

Tim Cook mentioned an idea passed down in the teachers' union movement: "Years ago some old-timer said at an NEA conference that in order to organize you need to talk to everyone in your bargaining unit and you can't organize if you can't do that. That was not our experience." While a worthy a goal, such a requirement proved false. This is connected to the finding that in the vast majority of cases, even a minority petition would result in a substantial election victory. As the movement progresses into organizing in the more difficult sectors, like for-profits and corporate contexts, this generalization may change.

When facing strong anti-union campaigns, organizers should not underestimate the employer's resolve to fight and use intimidation tactics. Several organizers mentioned that the best way to fight fear was to keep talking and maintaining contact with people, an effort that grows difficult in a long and drawn out campaign. Furthermore, it is a mistake to assume continued support without constant reconfirmation, and it is also a mistake to assume that friendly collegial ties to an organizer would immediately translate into pro-union support under employer pressure. Karl Black identified this as one of a series of mistakes:

> First, one of the biggest departments was computers. [The head of it] quit just before the first election. They elected a new head who was a supporter and that was the biggest department and I thought that was enough. I should have concentrated on them. In the first election they said to a person they would not get as much out of the union. I should have had more meetings with them. Second, I relied on friendships rather than treating it like a business. I had known [name omitted] for twenty years in life drawing and she turned on me. Third, I did not convince Tom Suhrbur of the owner's evilness. We tried to convince him but I do not think we fully convinced him. Finally, the fear factor was a major thing that I did not factor in enough.

One organizer mentioned that maintaining other pre-union forms of organization (college committees and other unofficial bodies) during the union drive and after the election was not useful and siphoned time and energy from valuable activities. Flo Smith from DeKalb said:

> We kept the Council of Temporary Faculty because we thought it was worthwhile. We had no voice in the University Council and no vote. That wasted a lot of our time.... It made us a little bit more visible but it got us no place fast. It continued till two years ago, then voted itself out of existence.

Others wished there had been enough human resources to do more outreach earlier, both within the potential bargaining unit and to potential strategic allies. Olive Light:

> Getting more people in earlier probably would have saved me from being so crabby sometimes. Building stronger ties to the clerical workers' union might have been useful. It has all stemmed from not having enough people doing the work.

Hal Jones from Metropolitan made a similar comment:

> The main problem was the pace, drawn out for so long. You would get tired after a while and not keep up on the contacts. You have to keep talking to people, constantly.

Organizing in colleges also requires an analysis of the entire political structure and all its actors in order to be effective. These include other unions, especially the clericals; the press, especially the student press; student groups; an analysis of the board and where power actually lies; the administration and its ties to the political community. Tom Suhrbur compared the campaigns at Harper and College of DuPage:

> Harper and College of DuPage differed even though [the district board had the] same attorney. We were naive [at Harper]. Our politics were wrong. We did not have our alliances. We did not do anything publicly.... We did not seek out the press, which is very important. We had no history there. We worked from scratch. At College of DuPage there was history, ...We attended board meetings and had a close alliance with full-time faculty.... We told them, "Don't pay any attention to your attorneys. Deal with us. We are the ones who make this place run. We are part of the system. Don't try to just use Harper strategy to defeat us because, while you might be able to do it, it is going to be costly and hurt the college and no one will be a winner."

How the Employer Responded: Although top administrators unanimously preferred "no union," they seriously underestimated contingent faculty's attitude toward education and their commitment to improve conditions by organizing. Employers largely ignored the campaigns, in some cases not even bothering to know they existed until the petition was filed, and in some cases restricting their response to a legal strategy.

Deb Brown recalled Oakton administration's initial disbelief, followed by stonewalling:

> The administration did not think much would happen so they didn't oppose [us] actively. We did not meet the same kind of opposition that, say, Harper did, at least initially. At a certain point, though, no more information was forthcoming. [The administration said] we aren't going to talk with you anymore.

Flo Smith from DeKalb reported a similar degree of disbelief:

> The administration did not know [we were organizing] until the labor board contacted them. ... They never called us. ... I don't think they did anything. I don't know why. I think they thought people were too afraid for their jobs and we did not have enough strength to pass it. They thought these people are just teaching on a temporary basis and they don't care if there is a union wage or not. ... They found out that that was not true. ... We voted in a building across from the administrative office and they stood at the building watching our people come in to vote for the whole day.

Sally Edwards reported that her supervisor called her and another organizer in and suggested that this was not their "wisest career move." But "otherwise, they pretty much ignored us.... I think he actually just felt that we would just go away. Fizzle and die. He was wrong."

The lawyer in the Harper case made a comment that Barb Polk, one of the part-timer organizers, remembered eleven years later: "Harper's lawyer was not a very pleasant person. He was demeaning and said the adjunct faculty were nothing more than little fish in the big pond."

Administrators also underestimate the potential backlash effect of anti-union propaganda, not realizing that it is perceived as insulting to the intelligence of the faculty and as condescending and degrading to their seriousness of purpose. Steve Jacobs described a campaign like this at Columbia College:

What happened was that the administration opposed us in a very stupid way. They hired an anti-labor law firm from Washington, DC, and put out the standard anti-labor stuff, which basically said you'll be folded into some large organization that will squeeze people and take your dues, won't give you anything. The are just out for themselves. We were able to combat it very effectively. They argued that you would lose your personal relationship with the college, as if we had one. You'll only be able to deal with the college through the union. You won't be able to talk to your department head about your problems or your courses anymore....We were able to turn everything back on them. They had said you wouldn't be able to negotiate for your own salary. This again was something we could point out—that there is a standard salary, that most of us got the same damn thing. There might be a few who could negotiate, but generally we just took what was offered.

Olive Light at Roosevelt described how the administration sent out letters in response to the union's card drive: "They were pathetic and if anything they antagonized adjuncts further." The letters addressed working conditions—access to copiers, office space, etc.—an issue the adjunct organizers effectively owned. Light:

I crafted the response letter and basically I said we need a copier to do our job. What do you think we are going to do, pencil these things in or run them off in our basement? Of course you need an office. Are we going to meet students in the bathroom? This is crazy. I think their letters probably helped us. They really pointed out the things that were ludicrous about our work.

Steve Jacobs told about another administrator tactic that was intended to divide people but in fact resulted in an organizing opportunity:

One young woman on the [organizing] committee had a side thing where she evaluated other people's classes. So they said she was a supervisor and couldn't be part of the unit and can't take part in the organizing or be part of the union. That made us pretty angry and we wrote articles about it. What happened is she would write stuff and have it signed by other people. Our lawyer told us that we could not oppose it legally. But we got around it.

Tim Cook told about a threat that backfired at Columbia:

They did say that if we had to pay $3,000 a course, the board of trustees might not want to hire so many part-time teachers and might make more full-time teachers, as if that was some sort of threat to us.

During the Harper campaign, taking the conflict to the labor board result-ed in giving the organizers an opportunity to confront their assertions. Barb Polk told this story:

> One of the reasons Harper said we should not be allowed to organize is they said we're temporary. We are like people who work for a temp agency who are in here one day and gone the next. Our point was to prove that that's not the case. I was the witness at the labor board and I had started teaching January of '80. This hearing was in November of '91 so that sort of blew some holes in their theory of us being here today and gone tomorrow.... One of the things that they asked me to display at the hearing was my fac-ulty ID card. Every semester Harper [had given] me a new one of these and I remember I had so many in my wallet.... Here it is 2002 and I am still there teaching part-time.

Together, these experiences suggest that if fear can be overcome, the employer's underestimation can be turned into a strategic advantage for con-tingent faculty.

The two elections lost were both cases where traditional private sector, for-profit intimidation tactics, not cogent arguments, seem to have played the key role. Tom Suhrbur discussed the harsher tactics at the for-profits:

> For-profit schools are much different from private nonprofits. [They have] different histories.... At small for-profits it is vicious, like a factory. They fired our leaders and we had the election overturned. It was a full-scale assault and was fairly effective. There is so much intimidation at the private for-profits. At AIT [another for-profit small art college where the campaign never really got off the ground] they started one-on-one conversations by the administration and offered people things. Several are owned by corpo-rations [that] own schools all over the nation. [We] have to build [our] organizing strategy around the kind of institution you have because each has different history.

Karl Black remembered:

> 1998 was the first election. [The president] had a couple of months to pres-ent his arguments against the union, so he had meetings everyday with individuals and groups and a constant campaign he put on. Letters, memos, on why we should not join the union ... They used the fear factor. "It could

affect your job." Told this to people one-on-one. The outcome was that we lost by one vote....We decided to [challenge] the election because of some illegal things they had done. ... Because we won the appeal, they were a little more cautious [in the second election]. They used more psychological fear: "The school may not be profitable if the union [comes in]. We could not sell it, and would just close it down." So they used more psychological fear, and it did work.

The campaign at Metropolitan was equally brutal, as Hal Jones recalls:

The National Labor Relations Board gave Metropolitan six months before they called the election. So we were under intense pressure. We were called into these meetings where no one could talk. They would give you all this propaganda about the union coming in. You'll just be giving them your money. They are corrupt. They will just exploit you. All that crap. Things started to happen. Like someone threw paint all over the car of the president. I never knew who did it. Things started to get tense. They brought in a black woman [as president] to bust the union, play it really hard. The new president would get in people's faces, call them in and threaten them. There was one guy who I am sure they were using as spy in the organization. Very two-faced... Finally we had the election and we won, but they had whittled us down to twenty-seven votes. In that six months they had scared about twenty people out of voting or the union. [The final vote was] twenty-seven to eighteen or nineteen.

In some cases, lower-level administrators, especially if they had been long-time faculty members and even contingent workers themselves, were sympathetic and quietly assisted the union or attempted to moderate the anti-union campaign by not fully following instructions. Earl Silbar remembered:

Where I worked the dean turned her back and let me know where I could get all the information I needed as an organizer. She had been a teacher and she thought it was terrible that we had gone all these years without a raise. And she was happy to see us get a union.

Steve Jacobs told how the Columbia administration drafted a letter, sent it to department heads with instructions to sign it, and send it on to everyone in their departments. Then department heads confided to contingents that the letters had not actually been written by them:

It was amazing to see how many just toed the line.... Then they would come up to us and say, you know, we are sorry.... Some of them privately confessed that, "Well, I didn't really write this. I don't really believe this." We were able to combat this very effectively and say who it had been written by and what the process was. A lot of people who had been hanging back seeing this—it brought them in.

In other cases, some administrators took this as an opportunity to settle old scores and get rid of individual organizers. They may have been prodded to act out of fear that if the union drive was successful and some degree of job security won, they would have to deal with this person in the future. Earl Silbar told of one firing:

> One of our key activists was fired by her dean, who was the person hired to clear out the radicals. We had picket lines in support of her but were not able to get her job back.... I think she was actually fired for using a loudspeaker to make an announcement about a meeting.

Olive Light at Roosevelt:

> Two people were officially let go and one "not reassigned." The university started cleaning house and the two people who specifically lost positions were in composition. Part of it was a conflict with a particularly difficult supervisor.... He decided he had had enough of them, even though they had been there for eight and six years. One had outstanding qualifications. She'd had personality conflicts with him over three years, and she was active. I think she was let go because he had seen the writing on the wall and saw that once the contract was in it would be a lot harder to get rid of her.

The union filed an unfair labor practice because, "The way he fired them was stupid, with a letter saying things he could not really support specifically." But the ULP was unsuccessful. However, Light commented, "that might be part of why he is not director anymore."

Organizing Committees and Who Leads Them: How we organize largely determines how our union will function later. Many organizers said without organizers who had previous political activist experience, though not necessarily union experience, especially having a broader, usually radical or leftist, social and political perspective some of these campaigns would never have happened at all. Others may have foundered, not because they were "defeated" but mainly because of a lack of energy collectively that could be marshaled over the long haul.

However small, a collective democratically functioning leadership, even if it falls substantially short of the 10 percent rule, can manage as long as the core group remains open and evolves over time, allowing individuals to drop off temporarily and others to join. Deb Brown from Oakton described having two circles: "A very small group doing the majority of the work and then a larger circle. We have always had a wonderful core, but it changes over time." Steve Jacobs from Columbia described a similar inner and outer group: "We had a group that was never more than ten people. Other people who did something were probably ten or fifteen more. It was pretty small—Columbia was 800 to 900 part-time faculty, then." But the quality of the core was what mattered. Jacobs continued:

We had a very good organizing committee—a lot of different styles. Lots of difference competencies. We had some sort of back and forth, and struggles. But we basically were able to go out and do it. [There wasn't] anyone who really drove us apart except for maybe one person who sort of split off. I think getting a really good nucleus is a main thing. When we met with [AFT leader] Mitch Vogel before we started organizing, he said, well, it's very obvious that you were going to succeed because you have a good organizing committee. That's key. It seems to me.

Whether this trend is specific to contingent faculty, the "10 percent of the proposed unit on the committee" rule can be finessed. Although building a 10 percent-plus committee is still a good idea, perhaps it is less essential among contingent faculty. Or perhaps the organizing committee should be redefined to include people who almost never see each other face-to-face but who work on an occasional or more regular basis coordinated only through answering machines and e-mail.

Taking on a leadership role in organizing can be enriching when they feel supported and appreciated by the rest of the core group and membership. For some, this was a confidence-building experience that reaffirmed their faith that "regular people like us can do something to change the world we live in." Tim Cook from Columbia told his own story about learning to take leadership roles:

Personally being an organizer was great for me. I was shaking in my boots at the beginning. I learned after years of writing, or maybe relearned, what I learned in the '60s and '70s, that you can do something. That certainly cheers me up. Also that you can exercise some leadership. I don't mean that personally, but that people who are on the right side of things can exercise some leadership when things are bad and you don't have to believe what the pundits say about the way things have to be. Things can happen and a small number of people can exercise leadership and provide a voice for the voiceless.

Flo Smith at DeKalb had to be talked into it:

Mike [the staff organizer] told me at a meeting: you need to be the president. I said I can't do that. I have kids at home and I can't give up all those weekends to go to meetings outside DeKalb. He said you don't have to do that. You can get your VP to do that and just run things on the campus. So [the VP] went to the meetings. I had no idea what I was to do. I was given some training, but I was a total novice. I did not know what collective bargaining was. I did not know anything about unions. [But I learned that] if you have enough people helping you taking baby steps along the way, you can do fine with the organization.

In cases of organizers outside the bargaining unit—staff organizers or full-time tenure track faculty who were elected leaders of a full-time unit—running the campaign, contingent faculty will not, in any numbers, come forward to build an organization and assume leadership if they do not perceive union involvement as a coming together of friends and colleagues collectively. Instead they would likely view it as joining an existing service organization, perhaps as a gesture of solidarity. In these cases the number of contingents being organized would not have been enough to change the balance of power within the full-time tenure track-led union. Unions have to be prepared to engage in internal transformation. Further, in the case of contingent faculty, if that possibility does not exist, the newly organized will not actively participate and therefore are unlikely to become potential organizers of new members themselves.

Attempting to find a pattern where committee activists come from within the university proved difficult. Those who faced fewer alternative employment opportunities outside academia seemed somewhat more likely to be involved. There are also disciplines in which a disproportionate number of women are employed compared to other areas, certainly compared to full-time faculty. However, this was not reflected in the composition of the organizing committees. Although some organizing committees were composed solely of women and although some women were self-motivated organizers, some organizing committees were composed mainly of men despite substantial numbers of women in the proposed unit. This points to confirmation of some of the findings in Sue Cobble's *Women in Unions,* explaining that the personal cost of union activism is higher for women than for men, because of the double shift that many women workers have to carry. That point is certainly supported by my personal experience in the various campaigns.

The same is true for racial and ethnic organizing committee representation . Steve Jacobs acknowledged that the Columbia organizing committee was representative in some ways, but still white, while the workforce was not entirely white:

Three from liberal arts, career teachers, two women, mainly male, mostly older, one young woman who was very involved and very central. Everyone else was at least forty. We had a mix of departments. They tended to be from service departments [i.e. general education] rather than the professional departments. The faculty was not all white but the organizing committee was all white.

Hal Jones described consciously strategizing around this at Metropolitan:

Our organizing committee was pretty collective, [but] I didn't want to take the real strong sole leadership, for two reasons. One was that I always thought that the organizer who does everything is not a very good organizer... And, as the only white person in the workforce, I thought it was better to have black leadership. In fact [the administration] did try to use that. I had a pretty good relationship to everyone and I was really part of the core but sensitive to not trying to use my experience to take over leadership. So they were not able to use that very successfully.

Contingent higher education faculty is still overwhelmingly "white," as is full-time tenure track faculty. However, in the Chicago area, there are substantial numbers of people of color teaching, who in my observation, have not been proportionally represented in organizing committees. This is an essential issue to address in any organizing plan.

Relations with Union Staff: Most organizing committee members felt positively toward union-delegated staff organizers. Staff organizers were perceived as being energetic, professional, appropriate (generally), and focused on the same goals as the organizing committee, namely building the campaign by involving as many people as possible. Even in cases where later relationships with servicing reps and parent unions turned ugly, the memory of the organizer remained a good one. Earl Silbar remembered that "AFSCME promised us a full-time organizer, who they gave us, who was very capable." Steve Jacobs remembered, with amusement:

> It was a good thing that [Tom Suhrbur] was such a good guy. Sometimes we would really sideline him a lot. We told him basically that you are here because we need the resources of the large union, but we are going to do this ourselves. He said fine. Tom kept trying to get us to do meetings, and tell us not to write too much, but in higher ed, people will read. You just couldn't do a lot of eye-to-eye, so you had to do this. If it's a crucial issue to them, people will read.

Olive Light echoed this: "Tom Suhrbur was the man for the job because he had an understanding of academia and we could identify with him."

The transition from relating to an organizer to relating to the staff representative who would help them bargain a contract and then administer it was often difficult and problematic. The general pattern of unions is to pull the organizer out as soon as the election is won and send in a collective-bargaining representative or servicing representative and shift the relationship to that person as soon as possible. This often left the organizing committee feeling disorganized, cut their efficiency, and forced them to develop a new relationship with someone whose view of them and of the task at hand was quite different from their own experience. This new person had not shared that particular organizing experience but came in with the organizational imperatives of the parent organization and concerns about dues, organizational structure, and bargaining requirements, which in many cases were at odds with the consensus of the leadership committee. The staff rep often carried a much less participatory, democratic, and experimental style. These problems were not universal, but seemed to revolve mainly around issues of respect for autonomy and a continuing focus on the importance of judging tactics by what would generate a high level of activity by members. Earl Silbar's experience with AFSCME in the city colleges provides an example:

> The organizer is gone and they send a council rep to replace the international organizer who is gone. The first thing she did was send a letter out to the membership, unauthorized, telling them what they were going to pay in

dues. We had been told you will *negotiate* your dues structure with AFSCME . ... Many of us were outraged. We said, "This is no way to communicate with the people who just voted for the union. This is not what you want to do." But it was indicative. The first thing to be negotiated was AFSCME's fair share.

As the Adult Educators prepared for negotiations, the issue of whether negotiations sessions would be open to membership presence came up. This led to a direct confrontation between the members of the bargaining unit and the staff representative:

> We had had a referendum of our members. Eighty percent of our voting members said they wanted open negotiations. In fact, we did have people come down and what happened was the council VP who was there worked out a deal with management and excluded them because he refused to certify that they were part of our bargaining committee. We had a confrontation with him. We said our members want this. This is going to strengthen us. People are going to see how recalcitrant and unfair management is and this is what is going to bring us together. They will see what we are actually dealing with. He said, and I'll never forget it, "That's what *you* want. I work for the council. We have our own agenda."

Among the important lessons here were the need of the rank-and-file leadership to take possession of their union and its direction and learn to do the necessary organizational tasks, including developing its relationships with state and national union bodies and with the college administration. The transition could be painful, but the sooner ownership is taken and relationships established, the better. Fledgling committees should also beware of depending too much on one good person either outside the union or within the committee, for if that person left, serious problems could arise. Hal Jones from Metropolitan tells of how their organizer and local leader died in the middle of negotiations. "It was a real tragedy." The local was then consumed by another local.

Deb Brown from Oakton spoke of learning this lesson the hard way after several members of the core group left and the staff union rep (William) came in as the expert:

> We kind of let William assume the leadership role that probably we shouldn't have. We did not know how to go about all this so we let him tell us. He had a thing with the [district] board attorney, Fred. They bargained a lot of

contracts together. Instead of learning how to do it, it was all, "I'll talk to Fred." It was seldom really positive, talking to Fred. But it was positive enough that we continued to let him do this. This continued a lot longer than it should have. I began to get pressure from other people that maybe William was not acting in our best interests.... At the end he was saying all these stereotypes about part-timers, like if you were any good you would have a real job. I don't see how someone can represent you and have those sort of attitudes. He and Fred would get into these things where it was really one-upmanship between the two of them, just male games with each other. So we got rid of both Fred and William eventually. I finally began to see that this was not the way things should be done. It took an awful long time.... William is now gone. He is out of IEA.

Similarly no one person in the rank-and-file leadership should monopolize the relationship with the union staff and the organizers, but that relationship should reflect the continuation of a collective leadership through the organizing period, the development of the first bargaining proposals, the negotiation of the first contract, and the institutional creation of the union in that bargaining unit. At DeKalb, Flo Smith said that the staff rep is "never chief negotiator; we always have someone in the chapter so we know what we are doing afterward."

Deb Brown summed up the lessons they learned at Oakton:

Learn all you can as fast as possible about how to do it yourself and do not overly rely on your Uniserv director.... I think it is important to get training from different people who may not say the same thing, different styles, explain things a little differently. Now I talk to others. I talk to Heartland, which is AFT, extensively... and to [the organizer] at College of DuPage.

Negotiating a First Contract: The first contract campaign should be viewed as part of the organizing process. Deb Brown explained: "Before you organize and bargain you don't have a relationship." Through organizing and bargaining, "you establish the rules that you and the administration are going to play by."

When asked to "tell the story," all organizers included the first contract negotiations as part of "the story," part of the organizing process. In new unit organizing, the first contract negotiations were characterized as being difficult and extended and not consistently conducted in good faith on the part of the employer. Deb Brown said, "They accepted the results of the election, but bargaining in good faith is a totally different issue. I am not sure the college has ever bargained in good faith." Hal Jones from Metropolitan commented, "They spent so much more money in trying to prevent us from getting a contract, that they could have [met our demands]."

The pattern that I have observed in my years in the teachers union movement was confirmed: when pressed sufficiently, employers were willing to make substantial concessions on pay, less on health benefits, but hold very tightly to all issues regarding power, flexibility, or the job security of contingent faculty. Earl Silbar corroborated this observation:

> In first negotiations, [the employer's] position was that you are part-time, at-will employees and we are not going to change that. You are not going to get paid for any time you are not in class. We are not going to give you any paid medical benefits. We *are* willing to negotiate your pay. We had to push against that. We have made some breakthroughs despite management saying they would never allow it. We got holiday pay, and we won a weird partial vacation schedule. They said they would never pay us for preparation time but we now get 91 cents for every hour we are scheduled to be in the classroom. ... It is something, in the sense that they said you will never get prep time.

Because of this administrative priority—to make concessions on wages but to hold fast on working condition issues such as job security—the adjuncts at Roosevelt dealt with working conditions first, and took some heat from their members for doing so. Olive Light remembered:

> We got grief from some adjuncts for not getting to money first. We felt we had to do conditions first because once we got to money people will just want to wrap it up and we will not be able to think out all these other things that do matter.

A characteristic argument administrators made against any kind of job security was that contingents had not been evaluated. Administrators blamed department chairs for this, but this only meant that an evaluation process had to be bargained. Flo Smith explained:

> They did not want us on continuing contracts because a lot of us were not evaluated at that point. They said chairs were retaining us because they were too lazy to hire someone else for that position. ... [Now] if you get a

bad evaluation you can appeal it. There is now a due process, reconsideration committee, and that has worked very well.

Frequently, administrators at first contract negotiations were often honestly ignorant of contingent faculty's working conditions and the treatment because of the heritage of the decentralization, verging on outsourcing, of much of the teaching function of modern higher education. In some cases, the payroll list was the only centralized data that the top administration seemed to have for its contingent faculty. Therefore, the first negotiation process took on, in many respects, characteristics of an educational seminar with contingent faculty asserting various conditions that they wanted changed, and employer representatives denying their existence until an investigation demonstrated that these conditions did exist. Flo Smith described how administrators had to learn about the range of pay contingents were receiving:

> They did not believe what we told them about salaries being hugely varied. Some were $12,000 and some $30,000. They did not believe any of that. This [had not been] a concern for them before. They had to get back to the chairs.... They found out it was true. When they found out they had some empathy.

Sometimes, employer representatives simply could not understand the bargaining team's priorities, such as those put forward by the union at Metropolitan. Hal Jones remembers: "Our position was that the biggest raises should go to the lowest paid workers, receptionists and staff, so that they could get off food stamps. ...They were just ideologically set against the union."

This process of reeducation of administration was tedious and frustrating for the contingent faculty bargainers, since as any teacher knows it is much easier to teach a student who is eager and enthusiastic about learning than it is to teach one who resists and denies every step of the way. This is especially true when the learners have power over the teacher and fundamentally think they have nothing to learn.

In several negotiations, it became clear that the more public and publicized the negotiations were, the better for the new union. Whether that communication took place by having rank-and-filers come to the negotiations, leaflets, e-mails, website reports, it seemed almost always to be to the union's advantage to keep its membership informed as much as possible. Olive Light told what happened when the Roosevelt contingents started regularly putting negotiation updates on their website:

In September we presented our proposal and put it on our Web page. One of the best things we did was using our Web page. That has been fantastically successful. [One of our members] puts everything up. Throughout the year we had updates on negotiations after every session. Roosevelt's lawyer remarked more than once, "Oh yeah, I was reading your Web page." I think no one read it more than them. They were amazed—why would you put this information out there? Our feeling was, they are there for everyone. And it's good for other adjuncts across the country if they see what we are doing.

Undergoing the process boosted the confidence of many organizers negotiating their first contract. All of the campaigns resulted in a first contract. For those who have had their professional and intellectual capabilities undermined, questioned, denied, and disregarded for much of their professional lives, sitting across the table from the administration, many times one's own boss, as equals is scary. Olive Light told the story of the moment at which she realized she was competent to lead the Roosevelt bargaining team to win:

I remember at our first session at Harold Washington Library. We were all dressed up. I felt like this is a serious thing and we are going to look serious. I remember I wore my nice maternity dress and my hands were sweating and I was so scared. I had never done anything like this before. Myself and their lawyer were sort of the leaders of the discussion and it went smoothly. I felt good at the end. Fast forward to a March all-day session at Schaumburg, and here I am with a baby and their financial guy is yakking on and on. It's beginning to blizzard and heading toward five P.M. I felt like telling him to stop going on and on about how we would like to help you. I realized my own thoughts were a whole new feeling. So I said, "Let's wrap it up." I am asking him to stop talking! I realized I could handle this whole thing and that was very cool. We got a lot of things.

Contrasting Viewpoints: One of the clearest patterns to emerge in these interviews was the consistent difference in perspective of volunteer activist organizers and full-time tenure track faculty and full-time staff organizers who were organizing contingent faculty. The key dividing line formed between those who were working in this sector and those who were not, the differences expressed themselves in full-timers' tendency to underestimate contingent faculty's potential to act, organize, and speak on their own behalf. In its most extreme form, this was demonstrated in full-time union leadership's refusal to organize contingent faculty at all, expressing that disinterest in terms of people "not being serious," either about organizing or as faculty, or, at worst, actively opposing the effort.

But even among those who were committed to organizing contingent faculty, a clear difference emerged. In general, those who were not contingents tended to view the difficulties of organizing contingents as flowing either from the faculty's personal motivation or from structural difficulties of their casualized state, such as moving around so much, multiple employers. Contingents themselves, however, always talked about fear as the most prohibitive factor. Stan Davis, who was a full-time faculty elected union leader at Elgin, one of the main organizers of part-timers there, offered an illustrative account of the structural difficulties of organizing adjuncts:

> It's an incredible amount of work, an incredibly difficult process, more difficult than anybody would imagine. It doesn't stop with the recognition. That is just the beginning. We had this fantasy like you want to get married and live happily ever after. If you have been married you know that that is just the very beginning. The biggest part-time problem is communication, finding a communications mode. One of our problems was their access to communications. We tried to get them e-mail, office space, mailboxes. We have adjuncts who never check their e-mail, never check their voice mail. In one case, the person is just a technophobe.

Kathy Moon, the full-time faculty activist at Governor's State, similarly offered a structural explanation for the difficult of organizing contingents:

> They are struggling. They may be at three different schools, so which one do you become active in? [They have] no loyalty to the community of interest because they are not part of the community.

These structural barriers have led full-time faculty and outside organizers to assess fear as a less important obstacle to building collective activity among contingent faculty. Tom Suhrbur:

> At Columbia one of our guys said, "I'm not scared. What are they going to do, fire me? I can make more money flipping burgers." Fear is not a major factor. In general fear plays a role, but not a major role in education

[because adjuncts] have such a loose connection with the college, running around. So getting people to commit the time is the biggest problem, more than fear. Semester to semester, jobs might change—so how much do they want to commit? It's very difficult, [because they are] pressed for time.

Contingent faculty themselves, however, almost never focused on structural barriers. Almost without exception, they saw fear, and fatalism, as the main obstacle to be overcome. Deb Brown, contingent at Oakton: "Tremendous amount of fear. I can't emphasize enough the fear. Even now, because our positions are so tenuous, because we have no just cause [discipline and discharge language in our contract]." Steve Jacobs at Columbia: "Fear, of course, is the biggest thing. I think it is in any workplace organizing, fear of losing the job." Sally Edwards, from Chicago State: "Folks fear retaliation, especially with the tremendous history here. But I always said, look at me, twenty years and I'm still here. I use myself as an example." Karl Black: "The fear factor was a major thing that I did not factor in enough."

Fear is closely related to isolation, as Deb Brown pointed out:

There was no literature about the part-time situation. We felt we were alone. People did not know what was happening anywhere else. We had gotten contracts from Washington and Oregon, [but] that was it and that was pretty far away. We had no one in the immediate area to identify with. People in general knew they were in a bad situation, but not aware this was a national situation.

Tim Cook related isolation to the fatalism that some contingents express: "Isolation is at top of the list: the sense that nothing can happen; hopelessness."

This significant difference between contingents and outside organizers represents strategic and tactical implications for organizing. This might suggest that people outside the sector are too quick to focus on those aspects of contingency that differ from "regular" employment and too quick to disregard those factors—fear—that impede union organization in most of the regular workforce. Many of these same outside organizers expressed surprise that contingent faculty respected a picket line or built an organization that they felt they owned. Stan Davis, at Elgin:

I was surprised that about half of the adjunct union faculty picketed with us. I really had no idea. I was quite surprised. I [also] find it amazing that we are able to get 90 percent of the eligible people to actually become members [as opposed to agency fee payers only].

Repeatedly, outside union leaders could not say how many total contingent faculty worked on campus or what percentage of those were organized, even in the baldest round numbers. Some, in my experience, admit to never having asked themselves the question. Another perceptual difference was communication modes. Contingent faculty were unconstrained by the received union wisdom. Some campaigns used extensive literature with long articles and newsletters. Others were almost completely literature-free. The contingent organizers seemed to be much more flexible in their approach than the outsiders, who wanted the campaign to fit the "proper organizing work" mold.

Keep fighting, don't let up, continue organizational activity, and don't be distracted by the bureaucratic entanglements that arise in relationships with administrations or higher levels of the union, contingent organizers urged. To the extent that these necessary new forms need to be "serviced" by the organization, they need to be controlled so that the central focus remains on mobilizing the base and doing the sort of thing that led to successful organizing in the first place.

In this regard, contingent faculty needs to be seen as basically the same as other workers. Further, the attitude of condescension toward contingents expressed even by the most sympathetic outsiders is a problem. Deb Brown, who is the only higher education person as well as the only part-timer on some higher leadership bodies, made a point of this aspect in her comment on FTTT involvement in Campus Equity Week:

> The situation at Oakton is still problematic. Even where both [FTTT and contingents] are organized, if the rep on the state committee is a full-timer, the part-timers are still "the others." It is a very pervasive feeling. I saw this last summer in Los Angeles [at the national NEA convention]. Full-timers were saying about Campus Equity Week that they didn't think they could do anything. The full-timers in their locals would not go along with it.

Building a Real Union: Building an organization after an election victory poses the challenge of fighting for democracy and power in union decision making, in the broader affiliate organization, and in relations with union staff. The claim that the new organization as "theirs" (or "ours") doesn't come automatically. Earl Silbar looked back:

> Now that I have been in this for a dozen years, I have seen different AFSCME staff reps play the same political role, to squelch the democratic, mobilizing, participatory unionism that the majority of the organizing committee organized for. This started immediately, as soon as the council stepped in and started to run things. And the contract is between the council and the employer, on behalf of itself and the local. We have the right to vote on it, but they are the lead signatory. After the election and the contract, we were deeply, even viciously divided. Many, many, many of the original people gave up in disgust. But we won some autonomy. We were not totally smothered by this stuff.

Maintaining a militant posture toward the employer after after the first contract is signed presents yet another challenge. Steve Jacobs comments on that time at Columbia College:

> The period after the contract was signed was a hard period for us. I think we have fallen into a lot of lassitude. You get so drowned in damned administrative stuff in administering the contract. The school threw in every roadblock they could. Things they were supposed to do they weren't doing. We had to come up with the list and keep track of number of part-timers and who is in the unit and when, people coming and going, what the dues should be and whether they had paid. We decided not to negotiate to have ourselves paid, although our rep thought we should. We should have and we are going to do it this time in negotiations. I don't know why we didn't want to then, but we really need to.
>
> We were really in a big swamp with all kinds of stuff. I know I had a problem as newsletter editor with the newsletter becoming dull. You know, get your dues in, blah blah blah. I actually quit for a year. It's hard to adjust to that no-struggle situation. In retrospect, I believe we should have kept the struggle heat on and been much more feisty with the administration because they fucked us over in a lot of little ways. We kind of didn't fight and didn't mobilize our ranks. They tried to suck us into an old boys' network and also stab us in the back at the same time, and they did it. That's a lesson.

Tim Cook, also from Columbia, expressed similar reservations:

One of the things I worry about is that we spend half our time collecting dues and sending out notices for elections in Springfield and things like that, forgetting about [our issues]. Or we'll talk about percentage increases and forget about these things. The union is more than just a money-grubbing organization. There is a lot of bureaucracy. I know because I have to do these elections for councils, etc. They seem remote to me.

Stan Davis, of Elgin, noted the difficulty among contingents:

Probably the hardest thing [was] what I call the post-organizing period. Once the bargaining unit is formed, what is the reality of life, day to day? We have found it's very hard trying to get adjuncts, because of their varying levels of commitment, varying levels of availability and orientation to life, involved. We have had, for almost a year now, one of the five Executive Board adjunct seats vacant. We could not find anybody to do it even if we appoint them.

Demonstrating a willingness to fight to gain and maintain the respect of the administration is essential. Deb Brown's local voted down a contract twice:

In one of our contracts we got very little and the membership voted it down twice. The administration said, "You have to take this back and tell your membership to vote for it." When we voted it down the second time even after the college threatened us, it showed them ... and changed bargaining for the future. I like to think that the administration had come to see us more positively. They had a dinner for the part-timers for the first time.

Earl Silbar echoed the need to earn respect throughout the institution through militancy:

Now we have a new leadership and we are organizing the membership to prepare for a strike and damn the council if they get in our way. ... Our activists, especially some very strong women, have won a lot of respect among the credit teachers, [although] not their union leadership, who have refused to collaborate with us. We also have respect from the new leadership of the clerical workers. In that sense we have more allies and strength than we used to have.

Maintaining respect occurs when you keep at it, and relate honestly to the members. Even if they make mistakes, they will build respect from their members to the administration.

Paid negotiated release time and for fair share, contribute to maintaining a strong union among this relatively unstable group. Tom Suhrbur said among the lessons to be learned from these campaigns are:

> Lessons: the biggest long-term concern is the viability of organization because of the nature of part-time work. There is high turnover so constantly training and building leadership is crucial to success. You can get a contract, but can you sustain the organization over the years? So fair share is crucial. It is in the college's interest to do it, too.

Finally, fear still dominates contingent unions even after the contract is signed and the building process begun, for despite a contract, fear of retaliation for activism poses a real barrier many find difficult to overcome.

Future Strategies, Visions, and Goals: The overarching question remains: what is the larger strategy for contingent faculty. As Kathy Moon at Governor's State noted earlier, the reality of working at several institutions to patch together a livable income disperses the energy and commitment they can give to a single institution. But contingents themselves saw this dispersion as foreshadowing a solution: all saw potential in a metro-wide organization. Some saw it as a means of gaining health insurance, publicity, and a sense of a movement that could encourage further organizing. Steve Jacobs, for example, said:

> The most important thing now is to get enough schools organizing in order to form a Chicago organization. That is where you can tap the issue of health insurance. We tried to get that *Adjunct Advocate* [a national magazine with a linked membership group that offered a health plan] thing and that did not work. That has been our biggest bargaining failure. We have to find some way to get something set up that will work. Then say we want the administration to pay for part of it. If we could have a joint IEA-IFT thing and set up a group that would include all the Chicago area part-timers, then we could do something. I really think that's crucial right now.

Tim Cook expressed reservations:

> I feel mixed toward a metro strategy. It has some uses but I can't see using it to getting to a contract. It's a strategy that is useful for doing health insurance.... A hiring hall, potentially, and retirement makes sense, and publicity and education on a metro level make sense. There are a lot of connec-

tions to be made. We all know lots of other institutions and we probably cover them all and maybe there are ways to sort it, but I can't see organizing on a metro level on the same level [as health insurance, hiring, retirement, etc.] But when I think about the sense of isolation and the sense of not being able to do anything, we really need that sort of thing and models.

Some saw a metro strategy as a more visionary way to build a membership organization that could go beyond the limitations of bargaining unit unionism. Tom Suhrbur:

Tremendous momentum can be built up because people work in other places. Every victory can lead to more. You have to have a long-term strategy to commit to do that and create an area-wide organization than can sustain the part-time effort. You have to look at some sort of hiring hall that can set up a website, [keep track of or establish] credentials, rate colleges, maybe even [offer] a Taft-Hartley health care program. Build critical mass to force colleges to work together. The building trades have done it. In the building trades they forced employers into organizing themselves. Before, the contractors said, "I would love to give you more but if I do my competitor will under bid me and I go out of business." The carpenters then organized all the carpenters and said, "You'll have no one if you don't organize and bargain with us." This is the same kind of strategy. Organize as many as possible to get health care and pensions, public and private employers both. If you could get the Chicago City Colleges, Harper, College of DuPage, other community colleges plus a couple of universities like De Paul, Loyola, University of Illinois, you could really start to have an impact, much bigger than we have now. The key is to continue to organize and have commitment to it. The key is always momentum, either moving ahead or moving back. Momentum is crucial.

Tim Cook spoke about the need for unions to fight to make the distinction between contingent faculty and regular faculty "look silly":

Part-time faculty can be brought into the middle class in the economic sense and that's important. [Unions] should ... ultimately break down the barriers between part-timers and full-timers. I think that is a proper goal.... The goal is to build unions, and a level beyond unions. They exercise power on behalf of lots of things beyond their narrowest interests. They aren't a force for revolution, but to make society reorganized in a more democratic way we need a lot more of them. They are part of that. I am very impressed by the former Columbia president's comment that if all part-timers were paid $3,000 per course the board of trustees might have another look at the issue of use of part-time faculty.... What unions can do is put some muscle into moving in that direction. We can move to a point where the distinction between part-time and full-time starts to look really silly. After that, I don't know. Maybe then we have to step outside the union.... There might be some way to bring part-time and full-time together without the union becoming obsolete. I am still enamored of the participatory and syndicalist idea and democratic possibilities. The academic guild that includes only some people at the top is essentially exclusionary, a sort of parliament [as it was in] 1450 or something, not a real democracy. To create a real democracy seems to me a reasonable goal.

Even with differences in strategic clarity, the activists were all infused with hopefulness. The lesson of the experience was, "You are better off if you stand up for yourselves, even though you may lose sometimes." This rock-bottom antidote to the fear and fatalism that most saw as the key obstacles is perhaps the most important strategic building block for any future movement. Hal Jones:

I have found out throughout my working life that the more you stand up for yourself, the more they leave you alone ... They go after weak people, people on the fence. You have to be strong about it and you have to be sure you are doing your job...but when you stand up to them, they back off more than not.

Earl Silbar:

I was part of an antiwar group at Roosevelt University of seven people in 1964, and by 1966 we had spearheaded a movement that forced the university not to collaborate with the government in releasing class ranks for students to be drafted. I have every confidence that around work issues, class issues, anti-racist issues, that there is no limit to what we can do.

Black and women workers have tremendous potential in this sector and for the union movement. Hal Jones:

Black workers and women workers are the most solid political support for a union. Their whole lives [involve] dealing with racist power and institutions. They look to unions as something to defend them. Some unions have understood this. There is still a huge pool of low-paid minority and women workers in the country who have not been organized. That is where so much of the future of the labor movement is.

Keeping a focus on the classroom and the welfare of students and the educational process was an additional strategic lesson. This was seen as important for functionalist reasons—colleagues see this as important, and we need to meet them where they are—and also because it's right. Genuine effective concern and protection for quality in education can only come from those of us who teach the majority of classes. Karl Black, even after being fired and finding himself unemployed at fifty years of age, chose to end his interview not with personal complaints but with concerned comments on the quality of education:

> The problem I see is in the whole education system. This whole system encourages incompetence. The public does not know this. We need to have a hands-on look at what people are really doing in the classroom.

Lessons from Interviews

Without repeating the conclusions listed at the end of chapter 2, here are some of the most important additional lessons from the organizers' experience.

1. Build an inside committee first of all, even if small, and look especially for people with previous organizing experience of some sort. This is the core of the democratic collective leadership of the future union. Outside staff should be advisors, not leaders.

2. Nearly anything that involves more people actively is good. Welcome new people and try to model bold and committed, but not suicidal, behavior. This helps to replace fear and fatalism with hope and courage.

3. Learn as much as possible about the power relations and politics in and around the institution. Then look for alliances on and off campus, starting with our fellow workers and students.

4. All kinds of communication can work. The key is honesty, consistency and building relationships of trust over time.

5. We only lose, ultimately, if we quit fighting. Remember that the administration never quits

4

A Metro Organizing Strategy

Every situation is different, but it can be helpful to see how a whole organizing plan might look. One way to visualize the application of a metro strategy is to view it as a circle, with the top of the circle labeled "movement-building," or "the movement," and an arrow pointing clockwise with the bottom of the circle labeled "organization," with an arrow continuing back clockwise in the figure on the left. The idea is that an effective strategy must take the existing movement, build it, encourage it and out of it create organizational forms that can have more stability and institutional heft longer lasting than a movement by itself. These organizational forms should be structured and judged largely by how well they will build and rebuild the movement itself, hence the arrow back clockwise. Therefore this is a relationship that is both symbiotic and dialectical.

In a broader strategic sense, the proper movement-building, organization-building relationship can be seen as a part of a broader set of relationships in organizing that might be drawn as in the figure on right.

In figure 2, the movement-institution relationship is seen as a spectrum, with a second spectrum crossing it, labeled service-advocacy at each end. It

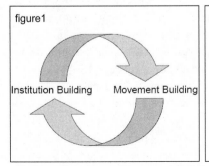
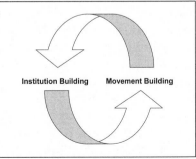

figure1

Institution Building   Movement Building

Institution Building   Movement Building

Relationship between Movement-Building and Institution-Building

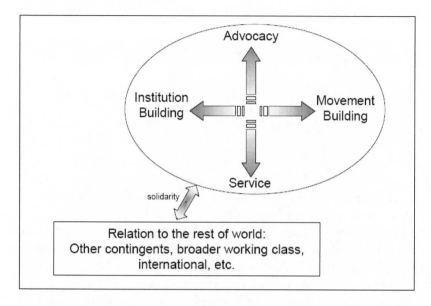

might also be labeled "individual" service–"collective" advocacy, though in real life these lines are not at all clear since collective service and individual advocacy are usually part of the functioning of a labor organization. The point is to highlight the spectrum of activities on the vertical axis and the future orientation on the horizontal axis. If one draws a circle around these axes, with an arrow pointing both inside and outside, we have the symbiotic relationship of solidarity to be built between the specific organizing context and the outside world, including all the potential allies from the campus to the community, from the local labor movement to the broader international working class.

Connected to these models is the question of "message." Since most of what follows will focus on structure and function of an organizing strategy, the content of communication should be briefly discussed. Decisions—on which issues to be raised and how they are communicated—should be the result of democratic and bottom-up decision making. That said, unifying issues should be the emphasis, such as respect, job security, living wages and benefits, and equity (with FTTT) in all things. For instance, the re-creation of FTTT jobs with a priority of hiring present contingents is a demand that is not of great concern to some contingents, but it is important to others. Therefore, it should be raised as a secondary demand. FTTT faculty should be encouraged to fight for this, since it is in their interest to retain and increase the ranks of FTTT faculty. Finally, the message chosen should be projected broadly, to the whole sector, public and private, by, what I will call, the Metro Strategy Organization (the MSO, a term for our proposed group). Slogans such as: "Does any adult call you 'teacher'? Join the MSO," might be useful for broad outreach.

Research

One of the first tasks for a regional strategy is to build on existing research to produce a clearer and more complete picture of the workforce, the employing institutions, and the political economic context. This could develop into a contingent faculty think tank that could conduct all of the aspects of research detailed below, both for internal uses and for external public release of "white papers" and other publicity. This research should be conducted by a combination of professional researchers, including people from local labor education programs and activists engaging in participant action research (PAR). As noted, contingent faculty are skilled researchers who could be mobilized for this task, especially if stipends were available. The gathering of such data would be useful for organizing and building the movement by involving more people. This plan would also offer a scholastic opportunity for contingent faculty to use hard-won skills and painfully gained knowledge to advance knowledge for a respected collective effort.

Research would include accurate counts of existing contingent faculty; information on existing pay, benefits, and other conditions of employment; development of a contract bank of contingent faculty collective agreements; analysis of institution-specific characteristics of the contingent faculty labor force, such as informal levels of organization, concentrations of activists, turnover rates, particular disciplines or fields and programs (credit transfer, vocational, adult education, continuing education, contract ed, corporate ed, etc.) that employ many or few contingents; and collection of demographic data to compare the differences and similarities of contingent faculty conditions across the area and within institutions.

Research of employing institutions and the associations among them is another avenue of inquiry. This would include study of informal and formal institutional power structures; profile of the student body, student organizations, or history of student activism; legal ownership and control of the institution; funding sources; major contractors and vendors; major sources of contracts; institutional history; past and present labor relations, past and present unions; and personal histories of leading administrators, "owners," and board members. This could be considered reverse strategic planning, or SWOT (strengths, weaknesses, opportunities, and threats) analysis. Luckily, recent literature on corporate campaigns and corporate campaign research would reduce this effort considerably. However, the unusual fact of our employers falling within all three major economic sectors—public, private nonprofit, and for-profit institutions—make tracking the funding sources and instructor counts complex.

Another focus of research is to assemble collections of journalistic and other published pieces on contingent faculty, their work, and the implications of the change in the employment situation in higher education. Such a collection has a number of advantages. First, literature could be assembled as orientation packets for new activists, sympathetic full-time faculty, and other potential allies, journalists, and legislators. This collection, which might also include some of the book and monographic literature on the subject, could be the core of a contingent faculty library or resource room, which would be of value to the movement internally as well as a resource advertised externally. Such a resource center would also be linked to any labor education efforts that were developed later on, providing some of the raw material that could be used for curriculum. This resource might expand into examination of contingent workers generally and come to play a direct role in a broader coalition, perhaps as a local node of the North American Alliance for Fair Employment (NAFFE) network, such as the multiple Chicago affiliate groups.

Obviously, another major area of research is to assemble lists of contingent faculty with as much complete personal data as possible, both home and employment, and to update that list to a high level of accuracy over an extended time. This list has two major uses. One would be as a database of activists or potential activists who can be called upon for assistance when a need or activity arose that matches their availability and interest. Second, the list would include all of those actually working in the sector and, as time passed, those who had worked in the sector and might well return.

In addition, a continuing effort, through interviews and documents, to develop a more complete view of the history of organizing campaigns and the people who led them has a number of uses. Many of the people who were involved can be reactivated if approached in the right context. The mining of this data can further produce and refine information, knowledge, and lessons to help guide subsequent organizing. The compilation of such a history, in various forms—perhaps ultimately as a short book, pamphlet, or video, could serve useful organizing and educational purposes, especially in conjunction with the other resources gathered in the resource center mentioned above.

Bringing together the best information existing on the legal status of bargaining rights and organizing protections and on contingents' individual and collective rights as employees is another research area. This should include keeping up on the changing legal climate on contingents' rights to "concerted activity for mutual aid and protection" in the NLRA, even for those not currently represented by board-certified unions. Because the legal environment both for organizing and for maintaining the rights of employees is a matter of active litigation and legislation that is unlikely to slow anytime soon, this effort must be ongoing. Based on the demographic data assembled, legal research should also investigate possible civil rights violations when discrimination against contingents constitutes discrimination against women or other legally protected groups.

In all of these research functions, in addition to utilizing principles of coordinated participant action research, the project should build alliances and relationships that will be needed in other aspects of the work. Included especially here are other contingent worker groups, national and local, and all unions and other employee organizations at any institutions employing contingent faculty. The general rule here is that research should be approached not primarily as a technical function, but as an organizing function, subject to the same goals, constraints, and allocation of resources as any other aspect of organizing. If data is gathered at the expense of hurting future sources of solidarity internally or externally, then the research is counterproductive.

A Contingent Faculty Center: Virtual and Actual

One of the most encouraging aspects of recent organizing research and practice in the United States has been the rise of the workers' center as a focal point for organization of workers, a way for them to come together and collectively speak to a wider range of their needs as working people in their communities. An updated version of a workers' center for contingent faculty can aid in communication and social interaction and can serve as a site for organizing, building solidarity, education, and provision of services.

The Virtual Center: Given the fragmented existences of contingent faculty members and computerized communication technology, a virtual center can be part of a physical center. Recent organizing in Chicago has shown that Web pages, e-mail, a cyber version of a printed newsletter, and listservs can fill communications gaps that otherwise might be difficult to overcome. That nearly all contingent faculty today possess e-mail accounts allows for a virtual participatory democracy. Perhaps this is the completing of the circle from the days when most workers lived within walking distance of their work and of their meeting halls, where they could meet to make the decisions. This virtual center could also be a vehicle for many direct services, which I will discuss in the next section. However, a virtual meeting place should never be seen as replacing the actual face-to-face contact that any activist organization needs to survive, grow, and exercise influence. Collective action is the only counter we have for the big money of our opponents. .

The Physical Center: The physical center would likely open first in a near downtown location, with satellites in other places as the movement progresses. The center would be equipped with fax machines, computers for secure e-mail, Web access, phones, printers, copy machine, and a package drop-off for deliveries. Because many contingent faculty lack free and easy access to such amenities, are extremely restricted in their on-campus use, or can't afford to maintain full home offices, the provision of services at the center may draw them to the facility.

The physical center would also serve as an office for the organization and staff, a place where files are kept centrally, databases maintained and updated, and phone calls made. However, this function of the center should never become primary. If it becomes mainly the "office" of the organization and the habitation of staff people, then it has lost its most important characteristic. We have seen this unfortunate transition before, as many "union halls" have become exclusively staff offices with no real place for members.

The physical center could be a place for the production of a periodic newsletter and the production of types of literature. It could be a site for meetings of medium or small size with facilities for light cooking and food storage. The center should offer some provision for child care since many contingent faculty, especially women, are harried parents.

A social center is a physically safe place where contingent faculty can come together and talk without fear. Very little of the literature on contingent faculty fully acknowledges this aspect of their lives and needs, except for the memoir horror stories contingent faculty have written. An open door to socializing would be maintained for organized and formal social events. Labor education courses could be offered. It is one thing to go to on-campus professional development workshops, but it is another to assemble a group for discussion and learning based on their status as contingent workers and a workers' organization in an employer's facility. My experience with this very fearful contingent faculty group and as a labor educator confirms that an off-campus site for labor education is essential to stimulate broad discussion and to cultivate much-needed leadership. This could be a central clearinghouse for information about the movement locally and nationally. Information here could serve to connect contingent faculty to the broader labor movement and the use of local labor education programs, contributing to broader solidarity and consciousness.

Finally, this site would be a node of solidarity for meetings and as a place for planning actions by the organization. Others in the community, in the labor movement, on campuses, and the press would come to know it as the place where the new majority college teachers could be contacted for information or for assistance. As the movement develops, there are undoubtedly other functions that a center such as this will offer.

Services

Essential to successful mass organization and especially union organization is the integration of individual and collective services if the goal is to have a membership and an activist core that is fully representative of the workforce. These services generally fall into two categories: professional and personal.

An initial service could be creating a job bank by soliciting (and pressuring) as many employers as possible to list all their openings, contingent and tenure track, for access by members. As strength is gained and leverage is accumulated, such a bank could evolve into a hiring hall with referral agreements from employers. The center would also provide a collection of ratings and reports on the conditions in various schools and departments as a guide for contingent faculty applying for work.

Professional development classes, especially those that focus on pedagogy, are another service. Much of the recent work in adult education and related fields remains hidden from the vast majority of college teachers, and classes can enrich people's professional lives, enhance their teaching, and provide a coming together that could result in a more collaborative teaching environment for many of the members. It could result in the creation of a professional teaching network from the base up rather than controlled by FTTT faculty and employers. More professional services could include assistance in preparing portfolios and CVs, a listing of people available for work, along with their credentials and fields, a listing of people available for substituting, a member directory, and assistance in attending conferences in one's field.

Under the category of personal services, clearly the most pressing is to collect a sufficiently large group to gain health and retirement benefits as well as traditional supplements to salary that are enjoyed by regular employees. In the short term, up-to-date listings and referrals to free, inexpensive, or sliding scale health services would be an assest to a great many of our members. In the long run, the effort would be to provide health insurance, either through a Taft-Hartley trust with multiple employers signing on or through other sorts of provisions. This would also be a major organizing magnet for drawing people into membership. Additionally, this can spark political pressure for national health care. Most contingent faculty already believe that health care should be severed from employment if true universality is to be achieved.

Helping contingents file for unemployment compensation and, when necessary, helping them with unemployment appeals is another service. In Illinois, contingent faculty, since they are "without reasonable assurance of reemployment," are theoretically eligible for unemployment insurance. This eligibility exists anytime we are between semesters or if we have no work over a period of time, like a summer or a regular semester. We are also eligible if, due to "lack of work," we are minimally employed during a particular term and are making less than we would with unemployment compensation. We then have the opportunity to collect the difference based on a formula. The vast majority of contingent faculty is unaware of their eligibility to collect unemployment. Some are denied and could be given help in pursuing their appeals. In California, union-supported struggle for unemployment insurance has gained members millions of dollars in benefits over the last twenty years. The same model could be applied, at least as far as legal referrals, for worker compensation. Likewise, other employment law rights, such as OSHA, civil rights laws, ADA, and FMLA could be better enforced with assistance from a "Metro Strategy Organization" center. Provision of assistance and information on these rights could lead to organized challenges to existing barriers, such as was successful in a major court case in California in the 1980s.[1]

Without a doubt, other personal services such as discounts, buying clubs, group legal and child care services, credit unions, and the whole assortment of member services that many unions offer could be provided through the organization, either through affiliation with a national union or by direct negotiation by the MSO. Treated in the right context, these can be union-building services and not merely the development of consumerism or "ward boss" relations.

Assistance for Organizing

The main obstacles to self-organization among contingent faculty are fear, fatalism, and ignorance. The experience of the 1997 Teamster/UPS strike with its ringing public demand of "A Part-Time America Won't Work" and more important, its generation of clear majority public support for this basic equity demand, probably did more to revitalize the contingent faculty movement than anything else in the last decade. It not only generated massive positive publicity for the struggle against the inequities of casualized part-time labor but it broke down the feelings of fear and fatalism, especially fatalism, by showing a victory, and one that involved many of our own working-class students directly. As Barbara Wolf documented in her film, *A Simple Matter of Justice*, the UPS strike was a direct inspiration for the Columbia College campaign in Chicago in 1998. Drawing from this, the assistance for organizing that the MSO can try to provide should be directed toward giving people on the campus the confidence to overcome fatalism, the courage to act in spite of their fear, and solid information and previous examples to dispel their ignorance. What the MSO must do is give people a sense that they are part of a movement that is growing, developing, and welcoming.

Concretely, this means a safe, comfortable, accessible, and private place for people to meet and get to know each other and form viable campus organizing committees and a place they could bring the specific problems requiring action, long before bargaining rights can be achieved. Taking action would be easier with the backing of the MSO. We can look to the successful experiences of the Unemployed Councils of the 1930s, which served as schools for organizing and the lessons learned were later applied after workers found jobs. Some committees may remain minority unions for a long time and others may initiate bargaining campaigns quickly, but all need to be nurtured, assisted, supported, and educated in the metropolitan-wide social unionism embodied in this strategy. With such support, their ability to weather a long organizing campaign before gaining legal bargaining status is more assured. In this we have many precedents, but we have to look no further than many of the education union locals, which survived and grew gradually in non-bargaining unit status for many years, in many states, led by a minority of activist faculty committed to "acting like a union."

Specific discussion of how the services being provided can be used to build an organization would be an important part of organizing assistance. For instance, brochures that say, "Join College X contingent labor organizing committee and gain access to a job bank, discount buying plans, assistance in filing for unemployment, a listserv discussion including hundreds of your colleagues, etc." And in the future, health insurance and pension plan. General worker rights and labor law help could be available, as well as help in contract campaigns and other collective bargaining fights.

Another concrete assistance for organizing and one in which the metropolitan strategy has already demonstrated its effectiveness, in Boston COCAL, is to provide activists to staff picket lines, pass out leaflets, and perform other public activities that might be difficult for the committee itself to do in the early stages of a campaign. The ability to put a couple dozen people on a picket line in front of an administration building might make the difference between a movement taking off on a campus or not, and that was the experience in Boston. This is taking a page from the Jobs With Justice formula of "being there for someone else so they will be there for me later."

With a support system like this in place organizing committees would be less dependent on outside staff organizers, giving them greater autonomy to have a little more bargaining power when the time came to decide on union affiliation. The history of organizing in Chicago demonstrates that committees would be strengthened with this kind of assistance. Materially, this assistance could allow a campus committee to produce leaflets cheaply, on their own; to assemble a database independently; create letterhead, logos and buttons; and run phone banks. With such assistance local committees would feel less rushed and could function on their own without immediately moving toward affiliation, thereby strengthening the movement by allowing local leadership a chance to develop without having to compromise their authority through premature union affiliation. Enlightened state and national union leadership should see this independent movement and leadership-building as collective "union learning," advantageous in the long run since it makes for stronger local unions more likely to help with organizing and efforts elsewhere. This will become more necessary as the more easily organized workplaces are covered and what we have left are the more difficult private sector targets.

Regional Publicity

Generating a constant stream of publicity about contingent faculty, focusing positive attention on the organizing movement and a critical pro-"new majority" faculty view toward higher education trends would be another major function of MSO. As it stands today, if progressive reporters want to pursue this story, they either have to talk to a friend, acquaintance, or relative who is in this situation, or they have to remember which of the regional schools was in an organizing campaign, or the name of the union, and call for a comment. Or they are left calling the central offices of one of the major teachers' unions, which may or may not be responsive or well informed. So the first requirement for publicity is the organization that says, "Contingent faculty information HERE," and includes our take on higher education and all the issues surrounding it.

When events occur that affect contingent faculty, whether budget cuts, tuition increases, administrative restructuring, privatization, contracting out, and proposed mergers, the MSO should be in a position to issue press releases to a network of known media contacts and to the network of organizations that constitute the broader labor and progressive movement. The MSO should be in a position to put its own spin on events that are caused by the actions of contingent faculty, whether organizing campaigns, contract negotiations, job actions—particularly egregious actions by administrators that demand response—and legislative activities. In other words, the organization should be in a position to comment authoritatively—not in a sectarian fashion in competition with other existing organizations—but with its unique perspective, common to all contingent faculty, on all issues that arise.

Besides helping to build public support and alliances, news coverage breaks down the contingent faculty's fear and fatalism. To see their own issues in print, with their own pro-faculty, pro-working-class twist helps fuel momentum. As it is such articles are rare enough that they stir immediate comment and are just as quickly clipped and tacked on office doors and walls. Just as lawn signs in political campaigns are more meant to activate favorably minded voters than to persuade opponents, so the generation of publicity is to encourage, solidify, and embolden the ranks than to win over the establishment.

Generating publicity and internal communications is one of unions weakest points in their democratic processes. The fear of having a self-appointed "loose cannon" spokesperson say the wrong thing or go "off-message" is deep in most organizational leaders' hearts. The MSO should try to avoid that fear by encouraging and training every activist to be a spokesperson—everyone who can find a platform, from their classroom to their churches, to their extended family, to their neighborhood and community newspapers. If any group of workers ever existed who had the capacity to speak for themselves and be self-activated, contingent faculty has to be the one. We must aspire to that classic moment when a reporter or an administrator comes to a picket line or other action and asks, "Who is the leader?" and receives the reply, "We are all leaders," as described in Staughton Lynd's book of the same title.[2]

Direct Demands and Advocacy

Publicity and organizing come together most pointedly when the organization is mature enough to begin to make direct demands on area employers and on the political system. The regional publicity generated could shift public climate so that, besides describing the "plight" of contingent faculty, it would be possible to make regional demands on groups of employers, such as the private-sector colleges in Downtown Chicago. The dream of a mass picket line marching through the Loop, stopping at the dozen colleges within five blocks of each other, making common demands, doesn't have to remain a dream. A foretaste, at the COCAL VI conference in August 2004, was when the entire conference marched to five Loop colleges and gave each a "Contingent Faculty Report Card." This could be linked to a basic Bill of Rights or minimum standards for contingent faculty, such as that already developed by Boston COCAL, AFT, and others.

These regional demands on employers could start with basic services, such as sending all of their job announcements to the organization, then negotiating an agreement to take referrals directly from the organization. The final step would be an exclusive hiring hall. Other issues would be subject to the standard-setting pressure of such organizational activity. These regional demands could be connected to regional publicity campaigns and coordinated with existing organizing efforts on particular campuses. The capacity to strategically plan such efforts and then execute them would be one of the major advantages of the MSO.

Publicly elected boards, other local officials, state government, and the federal representatives and senators could also be pressured. Given the difficult legal and political environment for organizing contingent workers, this is an arena that has to be exploited. Up until now, political activity on behalf of contingent faculty in Illinois and in the Chicago area has been weakened by the absence of a single organization or coalition that could speak with one voice. One example is the difficulty of getting the HB 1720 bill (on labor board coverage) passed with only one of the two major teachers' unions actively pushing it. Many other examples exist for which no activity took place because there was no pressure or no agreement. This solidarity in action in the political realm will only come when there is sufficient pressure from the base to force existing political and union organizations to drop their divisions and move together. This also has the advantage of being a political strategy that is not tied to a particular party or candidate, but is inherently issue-driven and dependent on mass activity at the base. It could easily be implemented through some of the vehicles used to pass 1720: petitions, mass card campaigns, public meetings on campuses, media opportunities, all with lots of opportunities for rank-and-file contingent faculty to be visible and heard.

Alliances, Coalitions, and Solidarity

One common regret organizers voiced in their interviews is their wish to have done more to build ties with supportive groups. Even the best locals become bogged down with the minutiae of their daily operations, college administration, membership needs, and affiliate commitments that development and nurture of relationships with allies goes unmet. So when the crisis comes, there's no one to call. The MSO can play an ongoing coalitional role for contingent faculty interests in the broader labor and progressive movement, even if individual organizations and local unions may have to drop out periodically. This is an aspect of delegated movement democracy at its best.

These alliances need to start close to home with other campus unions and organizations. This is where the shared interests of communities are closest, and the worth of a coalition strategy is most easily demonstrated to the average member. Here again, the Boston experience provides some examples. The University Organizing Project has brought together campus labor groups with students and political organizations to support organizing on campuses all over the Boston area among workers of all sorts, not merely contingent faculty. Likewise, the metro strategy embodied in Boston COCAL has led to participation by contingent faculty in the regional Campaign on Contingent Work (CCW), a coalition body of contingent worker organizations and advocacy bodies.[3] More recently, financial cuts at the University of Massachusetts were partially averted by an effective coalition of many campus unions. Contingent faculty played a leading role.

On the campuses, special efforts must be made to create the best possible relations with FTTT faculty and their unions. This may be difficult, but experience has shown that persistence can return big results. Alliances with other campus unions are often easier, and those with clerical, service, and technical workers are well worth cultivating. Alliances with students are especially important in this period because of the growing need and demand for higher education among students and potential students, who are faced with a difficult economy, increased tuition, and budget cuts. This can help unify contingent faculty and at the same time clarify potential alliances with students, other workers on the campus, and elements off the campus.

Another special effort should be made to emphasize the inherent feminist, pro-woman, and anti-sexist content of contingent faculty demands, given the disproportionate number of women occupying contingent positions. This means pointing out at every opportunity that differential treatment of contingent faculty is, among other things, discrimination against women. This opens the door to alliances with women's groups on and off campus.

Building alliances with working-class students, especially vocational students, is another opportunity to expand the network beyond campus. Especially now, with the proletarianization of contingent faculty, this strategic position opens up possibilities for alliances throughout the regional labor force in which the students will someday work. This can serve to politicize vocational students.

In addition, the emerging national network of contingent worker activists and organizations, especially under the umbrella of the North American Alliance for Fair Employment (NAFFE), can be exploited. This could lead to the development of a regional contingent worker network: for example, a number of unions and organizing projects in the Chicago area are already NAFFE members.

A final set of possible alliances are with organizations whose constituency overlaps with contingent faculty. Groups like the National Writers Union (UAW Local 1981) and other writers and artists groups, local professional organizations, even small business networks might become strategic allies if the potential membership is substantial enough.

Alternatives in Sponsorship and Organizational Structure

A key problem in any effort to organize an entire geographic area, even within a single employment sector, is the varying organizational interests in and around the labor movement that already exists. The difficulties of making one's way through the minefield of jurisdictional claims, historic prejudices, and simple parochialism and careerism are well known. A recent example of successfully overcoming these obstacles occurred in Hartford, Connecticut, where multiple unions have cooperated to organize the community's lower-waged workers, even through they work in different industries. Common issues included housing and the need for political representation. A goal in making this proposal to any organization or group of organizations is to maintain positive relations with existing groups and still sustain a sufficient degree of autonomy for the project. Any sponsorship or combination of sponsorships would of course affect staffing, budget, organizational structure, dues, affiliations, and other organizational matters for the MSO.

The preferable sponsorship for MSO would be a coalition of unions, probably the IFT and IEA and their national affiliates, perhaps under the umbrella of their national higher ed joint special project agreement. The AAUP and its Illinois affiliate might also play a role. Added to that could be the Chicago Federation of Labor and the Illinois AFL-CIO. A consortium of unions could then appoint trustees for the project but then allow sufficient autonomy for operational leadership to emerge democratically from the base. As bargaining units formed, there would be joint agreement as to union affiliation or joint affiliation, a proven option in educational unionism. Given enough political will, this idea is the most attractive because it provides the basis for the most substantial allocation of funds for a sufficient period of time to really test the model. This would probably take a minimum of two years.

A second scenario could easily be combined with the first or might be forced to stand on its own. This would be for the existing Chicago COCAL to constitute itself as the kernel of a new MSO and, through the auspices of NAFFE and its foundation funding and other contacts with foundations, establish itself financially on that basis. This does not imply that the MSO would become an independent union, but rather, through the exercise of ongoing solidarity, the project would develop positive relations with both individuals and organizations to make possible effective movement building. This would result in the growth of existing unions and in new units being created.

A less attractive alternative is that this project would be taken on independently by IEA/NEA or by IFT/AFT. (I assume that AAUP is not a possibility since it has a limited organizational strength in the Chicago area and no existing bargaining units.) This would probably mean less funding, more sectarian inter-organizational difficulties, and virtually ensured contested elections down the road and organizational activities not geared toward broader movement-building.

It is possible that the national AFL-CIO might, through its organizing department, be prevailed upon to exercise some influence here, given the substantial size of this sector nationally and its potential for organizing in the relatively near term. Serious AFL-CIO support would make a crucial political difference, not only with the state and local federations of labor, but perhaps in being an "honest broker" vis-à-vis the teachers' unions. A structural question concerns the acceptance of organizational membership by individuals before collective bargaining is achieved. Whether membership is in MSO alone or also in affiliate unions, how much the dues will be, how they will be collected are all matters subject to negotiation. "Open source unionism" or "minority unionism" is a way for the labor movement to rebuild itself. If the only way to organize is to wait to clear the legal barriers to majority-status exclusive representation, then it is unlikely that it will happen in our lifetimes. In education especially, the heritage of minority or non-bargaining unions is strong, and we should build on it and learn from it.

5

Getting Down to Work: An Organizer's Toolbox

So, you've decided the time has come to do something besides complaining or looking for other work. This chapter will give you the basic tools you need to get started. The first thing to recognize is that no one starts from scratch, though it often seems that way. We have the experience of thirty years of contingent faculty activism to draw from. Luckily, since this is not ancient history, many of the people and groups are still around to ask questions. Some handles to grab on to include websites, the periodic Campus Equity Week (CEW) efforts and Coalition of Contingent Academic Labor (COCAL) conferences, as well as many faculty associations and unions. The culture of the movement has been one of mutual assistance, volunteer labor, and a healthy understanding that a victory for anyone is a victory for everyone.

Just as every person is a product of his or her own individual history so is every workplace, labor market, and workforce. For us as potential organizers and activists, this is both good and bad news. The bad news is that our colleagues have many inaccurate ideas about our situation and what we might do to change it. Some are likely to be suspicious of unions or of any collective action that could only get us in trouble, and pessimistic about the possibility of anything changing for the better. Despite historic feelings of resentment toward working conditions, most employees are, to some degree, used to those conditions. There may have been previous efforts to get contingent faculty together, either alone or with tenure track faculty, that have left a few scars and resulting reluctance to try again.

On the positive side, this history that we all carry also gives us shared experiences that can bind us together. One of the initial goals of organizing is to open the door to some of those shared experiences. Contingent faculty is one of the most isolated groups of workers in the whole society. We work alone in a classroom or at a desk. Our very contingency means that many of us never really get to know or compare notes with our colleagues. Once we start, often in an organizing effort, we usually find we have a lot to say to each other. See how we aren't starting from scratch?

Even Two Make a Committee

Our years of schooling tend to convince us that the best way to change anything is to learn all we can about it and then write up our findings and conclusions in the most balanced, rational, complete, and detailed way we can. We have been conditioned to think that finding the full truth about something, whether in our own academic field or our employment situation, will make us free all by itself. Unfortunately, that is not the case. My father, a teacher for over forty years from secondary to graduate school levels, used to tell me that too much formal education tended to make people lose their common sense. He blamed formal education for the fact that it took most teachers until the 1960s and 1970s to realize they needed a union when most carpenters had figured it out by 1900 or 1910. The idea that individually knowing the truth would make us free, without any collective action on our part, was an example, to him, of that loss of common sense. Luckily, even the "overeducated" can still learn, albeit sometimes painfully and slowly. The key to this learning is doing it together.

So, your first step is not to study and write an article. The first step is to find a partner. Combining efforts with another person is much more than doubling your own power and resources. You not only generate ideas and energy from another person, you start to build the base for a worker organization, mutual help and solidarity between fellow workers. This relationship is what makes it possible to keep going when we're discouraged, helps us avoid the mistakes we can make when angry or afraid, and gives us a wider network of people to relate to than any of us have individually. Your second step is to form a committee, even if only a committee of two. The failure of many of our colleagues to understand this is one reason why more has been written about our situation than has been done to change it. Helena, my spouse and (non-tenure track) colleague, tells the story of how, soon after she got actively involved in her AFT local as a California community college part-time English teacher and writer, she was told by one of her mentors, "Writing is not organizing." It took her a while to figure out what that meant, but she came to embrace it. Of course, we do need to write: articles, newsletters, books, leaflets, picket signs, e-mails, contracts, grievances, and even manifestos. But what moves people into action isn't writing per se but the communication that builds relationships and makes information meaningful. Writing is part of that communication, but not the only part.

In seeking a partner(s), you may find some surprises. You might find that the person who complains the most may not be willing to do anything. You may find your closest friend is not ready to take this step. You may find your first partner sitting at the desk next to yours in a part-timers' gang office or across campus in another department. You may find her when she asks provocative or brave questions at a meeting or faculty development function. You may find him through a letter to the editor in the school newspaper or through a friend who is afraid to act but gives you a tip that "so and so is talking some of same crazy ideas you are over in the business department." There may be a tenure track faculty member who slips you a note telling you that Cynthia over in biology (or theater) was asking questions about what rights we have as adjuncts. A contingent colleague may also work at a nearby unionized college and be interested in organizing. The key is to find someone to start. Now you have a committee and you can start to plan how to move, which means finding other people, developing issues, and educating yourselves.

When to Go Public: You may ask why I have not suggested putting out a general notice, in mailboxes, or via e-mail or voice-mail, to all your colleagues and see who responds. Among the reasons to avoid this, as a first step, is that it exposes you, if you sign the notice, at a time when you cannot be sure how the administration will respond. But don't let that keep you from moving forward. Let it make you properly cautious. You won't be nearly as effective if you don't get any classes next semester. The second reason to wait on the broad-scale notice is that you would be alerting the administration that someone is starting an effort to get people together. Why give them extra time to plan their strategy? Your inside advantage is that you already know people, and can meet more, with some credibility as a fellow teacher. You can meet people "below the radar." Hired staff organizers coming into a workplace have no choice but to try to find people from the outside, which may include putting out a notice and then seeing who responds. Maybe no one does. The outside organizers are safer because they can't be fired, but they have limited access and knowledge about an institution. General notice will come when a committee has sufficient numbers to launch a joint effort.

Your Right to Organize: The most important point about the law is that the law is not the last word. First, labor law is constantly changing through amendments, court decisions, and changes in administrative regulations. In some states, provisions cover employee rights in state universities and colleges are in the general education laws. Higher education is covered by a variety of labor relation laws. So check out your current legal rights to organize for your local situation.

Second, organizing is not a product of the law, rather the reverse. Unions existed, even in higher education, long before enabling legislation did. Although it's better if we have a good legal climate, historically the laws came after workers chose to organize and became strong enough to disrupt the employer's ability to make money. When that was demonstrated by the mass strikes in the early 1930s and by the wave of public employee strikes in the 1960s and 1970s, laws were passed to provide a mechanism for settlement of disputes and the maintenance of labor peace. But the organizing came first. While our tactics may have to vary depending on the legal or political situation, the general goals and strategies for organizing remain the same: A few people gathering, sharing experiences, and making a plan.

Private Sector Institutions: In private institutions, either nonprofit or for-profit, the right to *"engage in concerted activities for mutual aid and protection"* is guaranteed by Section 7 of Labor Management Relations Act (LMRA or "the Act"). This means that not only do you have the right to try to organize a union; you also have the right to engage in other collective activities, even if you aren't in a union just yet. This right is not absolute and is often difficult to enforce, but those interested in organizing should know they have the legal right to do so. Unfortunately, tenure track faculty in some private institutions (not the for-profit ones) have been judged by the U.S. Supreme Court (*NLRB v. Yeshiva University*, 1980) to be managers and therefore ineligible for unionization under the protection of the Act. Yeshiva does not affect us as contingent faculty, but in most cases it means we will organize alone rather than with our tenure track colleagues. Some administrations have told contingents that Yeshiva forbids all faculty unions in private colleges. This is a lie.

The core ideas of the federal Act, passed first in 1935, are that we have a right to organize for mutual aid and protection and to form unions of our own choosing. Further, if we choose to form unions, the employer then *"must bargain in good faith over wages, hours, and conditions of employment"* with a union that has demonstrated majority support of those making up the bargaining unit. Majority support may be demonstrated by an election or by voluntary recognition by the employer pursuant to a card check, strike, or other action. Legally, one cannot be fired or disciplined for exercising these rights, and it is an *unfair labor practice* for an employer to do so. However, in recent years especially, the actual enforcement of the law by the National Labor Relations Board, appointed by the U.S. president, has been very weak. It is best not to rely upon the law to protect our activities, but it is important to know what the law is on paper.

Public Sector Institutions: Many of us work in public, tax-supported, and state-controlled institutions. Sometimes the line is not so clear, as in some states where there are so-called state-supported institutions. In a few cases, an institution is both public and private in different subdivisions, such as Cornell University in New York. If you aren't sure, find out if you are considered a public employee. If your check is signed by a public official, you probably are.

Public institutions are governed by state employee relations laws. These state laws vary widely. Some are virtual copies of the Act, and a few are friendlier to workers than the Act. Many are more restrictive, with some excluding large groups of workers from coverage. Some laws also limit what can be bargained and most forbid strikes. Some twenty-odd states (mostly in the South and West) have no law enabling collective bargaining by public employees at all and a few have laws that explicitly forbid public agencies from signing enforceable contracts with employee unions. In no case, though, is it illegal to form or join a union. North Carolina tried to enforce such a law and the U.S. Supreme Court ruled it unconstitutional. Obviously you need to find out what law, if any, would cover your activities and how it has been interpreted recently in your jurisdiction.

Employee or Contractor: Some contingent faculty are not considered employees at all, but rather independent contractors. In general, if you work at the employer's place, under the employer's direction, meet standards set completely by the employer with little or no individual negotiation, have your work hours and pay set by the employer, and otherwise are treated like an employee, then you probably should be classified an employee. This means you should get a W2 income tax form to file with your taxes. If your employer is considering you an independent contractor, you will receive a 1099 form instead. Many people are misclassified as contractors by their employers because that allows employers to avoid Social Security taxes, workers' compensation, unemployment benefits, and many other rights that accrue to actual employees. There have been (successful) recent court cases against major employers, such as Microsoft, on this issue.[1] Some continuing education programs and specialized adult education programs hire people as contractors. If you find you are being called a contractor incorrectly, this could become a major issue to organize around. In any case, status as a contractor does not preclude you from forming a group, though it does place you outside the protection of the labor laws. Given the state of the enforcement of many labor laws that may not be a big loss. Many independent professionals and contract freelancers such as writers, psychologists, and even physicians are moving toward unionization. They are also pressuring for legislative changes that would clear the road for full collective bargaining rights.

Building a Committee: Finding People and Developing Issues

The real organizing begins when the incipient group of two, three, four or more meet and talk. You must get to know one another and build some trust. Part of this has to be face-to-face. One of your general goals at this stage is to enlarge and strengthen the committee itself. You do this both by recruiting colleagues to join the committee and by starting as soon as possible to act like a union.

To build the committee means to make it larger and representative of all the groups, departments, and programs in the institution and by building the commitments of trust and solidarity. Once you have a cohesive group, you effectively have a union and you need to think about it that way. It may take a long time before you are strong enough to gain formal recognition from your employer, but there is a lot you can do before then to build your organization and to win concrete changes in conditions.

Recruiting: Finding as many people as possible, by doing what you did to find your initial partner, will help. The committee should pool all its contacts and think about whom to approach first, keeping in mind that the priority is finding people who are trusted, are likely to become active, and will make the committee more representative of the whole workforce. It is also best if the initial committee members are people who are respected teachers. This helps protect those involved and it shields the committee from accusations of trying to protect "incompetents." Activists are likely to face greater scrutiny in their work. Everyone on the committee should try to accumulate lists of all contingent faculty from whatever sources are available. There may be a published or online directory that includes some or all of you. Get full contact information if you can, including home phones, personal e-mails, and addresses, as well as college information, including department or program, teaching schedule, and classrooms. You will end up using all of these at various times to get in touch with people. Ask friendly clerical workers for lists; good relations with secretaries and with their union, if they have one, can be crucial throughout the campaign. This is the start of solidarity with other campus workers, which we need to give as well as receive. Some public institutions are covered by a state Freedom of Information Act, parallel to the federal one, which means that you can get a list of all faculty with some contact information by filing a formal request with the administration. This may not be something you want to do right away since it alerts the administration to your aims.

Find out who has been involved in any sort of contingent faculty committee associated with the faculty senate, administration, or professional development. Many of these committees, even if they are non-union or are anti-union, are venues for people to express their concerns and are willing to put time into it. Many of these folks have ended up launching an organizing campaign. At this stage bring in people who will bring in other people. If your committee initially is all English teachers, make an effort to contact people in other departments. If you are all men bring in women. Make sure your committee represents all races teaching at your school. Committees that do not reflect the range of the people to be reached are vulnerable to charges that "It's really just an English Department thing" or "All old white guys." You are not just looking for people you like, but people who share your concerns and are not too scared to act. Don't let the fact that initially you are all white history and English teachers hold you back. Most organizing efforts start among people who know each other already. Just get started and broaden the committee. This will pay big dividends later when facing the administration.

Look for people who have histories of organizational activity to join your committee. Political radicals are often most willing to step forward, since they have a vision of a better world and not just a better workplace. They may also be individuals who have faced opposition in the past and are less afraid now. People are also valuable who know about creating and running organizations. They may come from political or social change groups, religious organizations, or community and neighborhood groups. For instance, in the organizing of meat packinghouse workers in the 1930s in Chicago, two of the most important groups of inside worker-activists were socialists and preachers from storefront churches.

Ask yourself, who goes out of their way to teach about social movements in their classes? Look at the class schedule for courses that indicate an activist bent. You may have to visit the class, since many adjuncts don't have their names in the schedule. Look for the person that others go to with questions or problems. That person inspires trust in some way and can be, or is already, a leader. Find out if anyone already takes responsibility for organizing social events, initiates team teaching, cleans up the gang office. Many of us know few of our colleagues, but quietly nosing around can turn up like-minded people in nearly every institution. Some institutions have a more repressive climate than others and it may take some time. Just keep good lists and notes so you don't have to do the same work over and over. Also remember that people and their schedules and commitments change over time. Just because someone is gone for a semester or more doesn't mean he or she won't come back to work.

Building Relationships: Taking Care of Each Other

Recruiting and enlarging the committee is only half the job of making it stronger. The other half is transforming it into a group that trusts its members to act together. This means people need some time to get to know each other. People need socializing time and informal conversation. We need to take the time to hear each other's stories. How did they get into teaching? What are they most concerned about? Ever been an activist before? Ever been in a union?

To protect our jobs or to hope for a tenure track job most of us have learned to watch what we say to our supervisors and to our tenure track colleagues. This self-control comes at a price. Once we create a safe place, a lot of pent-up venting will occur. Although this may be hard to listen to, it's very necessary. As new people are brought in they need to be allowed to vent too. Trying to restrict it is at our peril. The organization we create is not just a list of names, a treasury, officers and staff, a contract, an office. A union is the relationship among people that allows us to trust that we are not alone and can act together in solidarity. We are asking people to give some of their valuable time and take some risk for the common good. Few people will do this without some personal ties to the other member(s) of the group, and venting and listening creates ties.

Building and maintaining these ties is a bit like taking care of your family. We aren't expected to love, or like each other, but like a family we need to take care of each other to succeed. This is the reason for the tradition in some parts of the labor movement of calling each other "sister" and "brother." It matters. We will disagree; in fact, we need to argue, debate, and discuss a good deal. But we need to learn how to do it in a supportive way for the overall task we have assumed: improving our work lives. It will sometimes seem that it is too time-consuming to listen to the tenth stupid question or the fifteenth complaint about the same supervisor. Sometimes we will have to cut someone off in discussion and get to work, but we need to allow that person time to speak as well.

Often the feeling people take with them from the meeting will determine if they talk to anyone else about the union or do any other work. People have to *want* to do voluntary labor, and they will not want to if their colleagues on the committee make them feel bad personally. On the other hand, the movement is full of folks, including myself, who will tell you that they have met the best people in their lives through organizing. I met my wife, Helena, at a union meeting—she was one of the other part-timers in the room.

If you suspect that you should have a cup of coffee and check in with someone who seems out of sorts, you're probably right. The skill of building the committee is one of the main skills professional organizers have to learn. However, those groups that self-organize and educate themselves together at the start have a collective strength that no outside organizer can give them.

It often helps to collect small regular dues as soon as you have some stability as a committee and a name. It formalizes the relations among you, allows for covering necessary expenses, and symbolizes a more serious commitment. Some who don't have much time to volunteer will pay small dues, so that is a way to get positive support from a broader group.

Acting like a Union

Building the committee can only go so far. Traditional union organizing encourages committee members to begin to circulate authorization cards to build for a representation election conducted by the appropriate labor board. In some cases, this is the possible next step, but I am suggesting that it should not be. The experience of contingent faculty organizing suggests that what is most important is not winning a secret ballot election for union representation—we almost always win those. Instead the focus should be on building an organization that can survive a contentious campaign and strong enough to force real changes in compensation, working conditions, and the quality of education for our students. This is especially true for situations in which we are not covered by collective bargaining laws. There is no point on which we cannot force concessions and some sort of de facto bargaining if we are strong enough, just as our union ancestors did before the laws were passed.

How soon you go public with your organizing efforts will depend on the situation. But as soon as you have a serious committee, you should consider starting to act like a union. It is one thing to try to recruit people to something that might improve their conditions in the future but another to present people with a concrete issue that you are acting to change right now. It is fairly easy to get contingent faculty to sign a union authorization card. However, getting them into the habit of acting together to improve their situation may prove more difficult.

The best issue to organize around may have presented itself to you already: a pay cut, no raises in a decade, someone died prematurely because of no health insurance, several sections were just cut and class size increased, experienced teachers replaced by new graduates, no names on the class schedule. All of these issues have sparked organizing campaigns, but you don't need to wait for full union representation to begin to act upon them. Circulate a petition, write a flyer, start a one-page newsletter, send a delegation to an administrator, speak to the public board of trustees meeting if you can. Do whatever sounds like fun and what people are willing to do. The employer will probably meet with you if you have a petition with a number of signatures on it. This starts the process of recognition and bargaining in fact, if not legally. Even a few of you can start. Pick a name for your group early. This shows that you are organized and gives a little more legal protection. You will be surprised how little it takes to get some attention. Check out ideas and tactics discussed in the *Troublemaker's Handbook 2*, edited by Jane Slaughter.

Some people will be afraid, but remind them that sometimes being openly active and identified with a campaign can be your best job protection. Administrations often are reluctant to act against open activists for fear of unfair labor practices charges, which at the least could be embarrassing. Also, disciplining an open activist might spark backlash, which the employer may like to avoid. But if your employer is likely to fire people right away, you have to act with discretion and secrecy. The range of employer responses in higher education is very broad. The best protection is having the greatest number of people acting together. Nothing is a sure thing, except that if we act like a doormat, we will get walked upon.

Dealing with Divisions

Building unity is a key defense against efforts to divide. Therefore we need to plan how to overcome both the existing divisions and those the employer will try to fabricate. One of the first things administrators say when the subject of organizing contingents comes up is that we can't, or at least should not, organize because we have so many differences among ourselves.

It is true that we are a varied lot. We teach for a gamut of reasons. Some of us prefer part-time work. Many more would prefer full-time tenure track positions. Some of us working in other professions teach because we like it. Many more depend on our contingent teaching as a major part of our income. Some of us are currently graduate students getting teaching experience and supplementary income before going on the job market, many more of us who have our degrees have given up applying for tenure track jobs. Some of us are not very focused upon our higher education employment. Many of us see ourselves primarily as professional educators and/or academics. Many of us desperately need health insurance and other benefits.

These divisions of economics and personal situations are real and cannot be minimized. This diversity should guide our organizing efforts and cause us to be mindful about what we emphasize and discuss with our colleagues. Nevertheless, all of us, regardless of our personal situation, desire respect for the work we do and very few of us are getting proper respect. Respect means equal pay and conditions with FTTT faculty. Respect is expressed in more stability of employment and adequate notice of work and assignment. Respect also comes in recognizing the past work we have successfully completed by giving us seniority rights to future work and preference for tenure track jobs when they open up. It is also expressed in equal access with tenure track faculty to the support resources of the institution, such as offices, computers, mail, phones, audio-visual support, and clerical help. When posed in this way, even if every specific demand is not important to every individual, the issue of respect is important to each of us, and all of us can understand how it plays out for others under that umbrella.

Beverly Stewart, my current local union president (Roosevelt Adjunct Faculty Organization, IEA/NEA), says that we are the homeless people of the university. We are everywhere; we teach most of the classes. But we are mostly invisible, just like the homeless people on the corner right outside our university doors. All of us feel that to some extent.

There are other divisions that we must confront. Often, people in the sciences, mathematics, business, computer science, and some of the professional fields are treated somewhat better, even a lot better than those in the humanities. In many institutions huge pay differentials exist among disciplines, partly stemming from the pay people can command outside academia. The differences are less at the community college level and increase as you rise up to the most elite universities.

Our goal always has to be to equalize upward and not appeal to the envious selfish attitude that implies that taking something away from a better-off colleague will necessarily get anything more for us. It almost never works that way and only serves to build bad feeling. However, most core activists are those with the most to gain. We need to gather at least the passive support of the majority of our better-off or more conservative colleagues. We do that not by attacking them and what they have, but by appealing to their sense of fairness and equity. For example, some people in business, who are taught to be anti-union as part of their very discipline, come forward to help lead an organizing effort. Always leave that door open by creating a program and culture that allows all to get something from the group, but never forgetting that the goal is to equalize upward.

We are also divided into various tiers of non-tenure track faculty. In many institutions there is a growing class of full-time non-tenured faculty (FTNTT) who often feel more allegiance to the tenure track faculty than to their part-time colleagues. These folks often recieve benefits, year-long or multiyear contracts, and pay much closer to the tenure track range. They often fear losing their small advantages and falling back into the adjunct pool. Organizing, of course, could regularize these positions and negotiate how they are handed out and their pay rates. In other places, especially community colleges, there are large groups in non-credit programs. These folks are virtually all classified part-time temporary, even though they may work as much as a full-time teacher. They are often left out of even adjunct bargaining units, and their pay is usually less per class hour. The usual differences in pay or access to benefits often depend on the number of classes taught and the length of service someone has.

Defining Who Is "In": When getting all contingent faculty together may seem to take years, organizers are often tempted to lock in recognition of a limited group with an election and a contract. I encourage people to resist this temptation, despite support from the administration and from the higher union leadership. Although in some cases bargaining units expand in later years, it sets a divisive precedent for the organization. People inevitably begin to think of "us" and "them" and encourage bargaining to focus on those in the current unit, who usually are the best off to begin with. Those with partial contingent units usually have weaker contracts and poorer pay and conditions. Some state laws make anything else difficult, but we should fight for greater inclusion wherever possible. Often, those contingents with one class, or teaching non-credit, can emerge as valuable activists and leaders. Also, many of us find our status changing over time, and having people move in and out of the bargaining unit and/or union membership only weakens our common effort and confuses all concerned. The resulting divisions can take years to heal and generate whole new cycles of resentment and distrust. It also can become an administrative nightmare for a new union. Some schools have three faculty unions, each affiliated with a different national union, besides various unions representing other college staff. These not insurmountable barriers should definitely be avoided if possible. We should try for the broadest unity possible. After all, it is the only source of our power to change anything.

Race, Gender, and Similar Divisions: Since we live in the United States in the twenty-first century, we have to deal with both the heritage and current practice of discrimination on many bases. In very few places are there as many faculty of color as would be justified by either the student composition or the general population. Although this is partly because of past educational disparities, a healthy dose of current employment discrimination exists in higher education. Equally as problematic is that most of our "white" colleagues don't see it as a problem. In fact, many see affirmative action as the enemy of "white" contingents. Employers, and some white tenured faculty on hiring committees, encourage this attitude by privately telling applicants, especially for tenure track jobs, "We would love to have hired you, but we had to give the offer to Ms. X for affirmative action." If this were primarily the reason so many of us remain contingent, the percentages of African-American and Latino tenure track faculty should have increased. Instead the conversion of thousands of tenure track jobs into either non-tenure track jobs or, more usually, part-time jobs leaves fewer good jobs for qualified candidates. Nothing destroys a union or an organizing effort faster than racial divisions. The history of the U.S. labor movement is littered with organizing efforts broken by racism, often with the encouragement of the employers. Even administrators who are not heterosexual white men have been known to foster divisions along these lines.

Similarly women are much more likely to be contingent than to be on the tenure track. Some figures show an absolute majority of contingent faculty are women, while an even larger majority of tenure track faculty are men. It is also true that gendered employment discrimination is still a reality in most disciplines. Given these facts, the entire struggle for equity for contingent faculty can be seen as a key women's rights issue. Framing it this way can both help us gain allies and help to educate some of our male colleagues.

In many states, our lesbian, gay, bisexual, or transgendered (LGBT) colleagues do not have civil rights laws to protect them and many remain in the closet. My own experience tells me that LGBT folks are at least as common in education as in other jobs, though many still feel the need to stay in the closet. All of the major teacher groups have now passed nondiscrimination resolutions that include sexual orientation, but conditions on campuses vary dramatically. Since sexual orientation can be hidden, this makes our colleagues liable to pressure if their orientation becomes known. The best way we can support them is to create an atmosphere in which they feel comfortable coming out and participating openly as LGBT people. Any nondiscrimination clause negotiated or fought for should include sexual orientation. Also, we should be sure our "family" talk does not exclude those whose "families" may be different. Often this paternalistic talk presumes unequal gender and age roles, along with the *Father Knows Best* family structure. This effort needs to begin with the early committee.

Committees that accurately reflect the entire workforce is a way to avoid divisiveness. If all voices are heard from the start, the emerging leadership will more likely represent a proper mix and be less likely to omit the special concerns of the historically excluded. Although diversity in leadership and activists is not enough, it is particularly needed at the start. We also need to remember another basic principle of unionism, which is that the union especially exists for those who need it most. Past experience has shown that, given the opportunity, the formerly excluded can, and will, come forward to support and lead the common effort. The old prejudice that you can't organize women, minorities, or immigrants, or whoever, has been proven wrong by history throughout the labor movement. Just as we, as contingent faculty, are daily demonstrating that *we can be organized*, we must avoid discrimination within our own ranks.

Communications: From Office Whispers to the Internet

The core of organizing is communication. There is no single best way for communicating; we need to try everything. And we need to ask the people we talk to, on the committee and off, what the best form of communication is for them. Below are some tips, but remember that no advice is as good as our knowledge of our own workplace and the people in it.

Direct One-on-One: Traditional organizing wisdom says you need to talk with everyone personally. That is wonderful, but it may not be realistic for contingent part-timers spread among many worksites. People have been successful without intensive one-on-one. Remember that these conversations are golden moments. Use the time wisely when you get a few minutes to talk with someone and then make notes about the exchange and date. You can get a few minutes with people in their offices, at their classroom doors before or after class, or during their class breaks. Sometimes you can make a date to talk with someone later. Don't push people to talk in places where they don't feel safe. Be clear about what you want to talk about and what you want to find out from him or ask him to do. Do let him steer the conversation somewhat and listen more than you talk if at all possible. Asking questions is always right.

Phone Calls: Most new contingent organizing takes place over the phone. People are generally very glad, and surprised, to get a call from a contingent colleague who wants to talk about their situation. Very few hang up or are hostile. Many more are rushed or seldom home. My experience is that it does not matter much when you call contingent faculty at home. We reach 10-15% whenever we call. The only exceptions are Sunday evenings. If you do it then, be prepared for a few brusque brush-offs. Be very polite and accepting. Don't take it personally. Try to get people to give you a good time to call back. Again, have a goal, listen more than you talk, ask questions, let the person steer the conversation somewhat. If someone sounds like he or she might be an activist, try to make a date to meet in person. People are much more likely to do something if they are asked face-to-face by someone they know, however recently.

Sometimes a call is more useful if a letter for follow up precedes it. This has the added advantage of helping you check out your distribution system and mailing list. If you only get an answering machine, think before the call, "What is the clearest short message I can leave in a few words?" Some people will call you back. You may be the first person ever to call to talk about their job and listen to their opinions. Unlike most tenure track faculty, most of us have no organized collegial relations and we are desperate for them. If people tell you they only have a minute or two, ask your most important question and then let them talk.

E-mail: Most contingent faculty have e-mail. E-mail can be a useful organizing method if the subject line is crafted carefully so that it does not look like spam and is clearly relating to the person as a contingent colleague from the college or university. Do not send out too many mass e-mails—they won't get read. E-mail is best used after a personal conversation and a personal e-mail address given. No e-mail is totally secure, and university/college accounts should be used only with great care. Some employers have attempted to forbid organizing messages in their e-mail systems and have even tried to ban recognized unions from using their systems. Organizing activities should be carried out via personal accounts whenever possible.

Websites: As soon as the committee goes public, establish a website. It helps if you have someone on the committee who is either expert on websites or is willing to learn. But setting up a basic informative interactive website is not that hard. Recent organizing efforts have found a website to be valuable because people can access them on their own time and from a safe place. You can put a large amount of material on it for newcomers to update them on what was done before they got involved. Be sure your website has full contact information up front, such as phone numbers, for direct contact with a human being. Anyone who sends a message should be contacted personally as soon as possible. Publicize your website on all printed material and include a link to the website in all e-mail as well. Remember that a website is public. Assume that administrators will see whatever you put up, so consider what you say.

Flyers: There is no substitute for at least an occasional flyer. Flyers can be stuffed in campus mailboxes, mailed to contingents' homes, or mailed to their college addresses, but many will not get there if you do that. Stuffing campus or departmental mailboxes has its risks. We have the right to stuff mailboxes if the college allows material that does not relate directly to school business, which has been the case in every one of the dozen colleges at which I have taught. Another possibility is to send flyers in interoffice envelopes as campus mail, best a few at a time so as not to raise suspicions. In general, when using campus communications facilities, the best rule is to remember that it is easier to apologize later if necessary than to ask permission up front, which will usually be denied, at least initially.

Faculty will read longer messages it they are well written and relevant to them, but brief is better than long. If flyers have a consistent look and regular frequent appearance, they can become the beginning of a newsletter.

Newsletters: Start a newsletter if possible, putting it out regularly so people will look for it even if it is brief. Some groups are doing this through e-mail, but remember that you will never reach everyone by e-mail and it is much easier to accidentally delete it. Some unions have been organized largely with print, but the key is regularity. Also, have different people write articles; a newsletter seems more legitimate if it has many voices, and writing is another way for people to participate. Once people write public articles, they have crossed a line into public activism. Anything that might interest colleagues is okay, and humor is great—not all articles have to be critical of the administration. Articles on how we survive and manage to teach well as contingent teachers are usually welcome. Find that graphic arts teacher who will help with layout or who loves to draw (cartoons are wonderful). Ask for letters to the editor and solicit them personally.

Unorthodox Communications: Beyond standard communications are many other possibilities. One committee chalked up the sidewalk outside entrances just before a big college event. Buttons, if people will wear them, can be effective at the right time. Signs and flyers can be posted on all bulletin boards. Many will be torn down soon, but some will be seen. Some communications techniques meld into media events, such as leafleting events or informational picketing. Don't forget the chance to get free publicity at the right time in the college newspaper. Many student editors are sympathetic once they understand that most of their teachers are "temporary." Letters to the editor in student papers almost always are printed if from faculty. At the right moment, anything can be effective, from balloons to funny hats to buttons.

Analyzing the Opposition: Power, Politics, and Strategic Planning

Any effort at social change, if it is to succeed, requires confronting some hard realities. One is that we have enemies, not necessarily personal, but people and groups whose interests deeply conflict with our own. One of the best books on adult education ever written, by Michael Newman, is titled *Defining the Enemy*. As academics and teachers, we have been trained to think that logic and truth will win. But logic and truth only win if their proponents can organize enough power to make that happen. This can be a hard lesson for colleagues who have been trained to avoid open conflict and "power politics" in favor of talking out everything until agreement is reached. This training can be helpful when dealing with equals and people we share common interests with, but it is dangerously deceptive if applied to people and forces that do not have our or our students' best interests at heart. Since the class structure existing in higher education parallels the class structure of the larger society, we have to develop an appropriate class consciousness of our own. The current generation of trustees and administrators view higher education as a business, which puts them on "the other side of the fence" from us, not just because their opinions are different but also because their "business" of higher education works only because of our labor.

Given this reality—that the folks running higher education today have different interests, as a group, than we do—we need to understand as much as we can about the power they hold and how they use it. We especially need to figure out the power structure of our own institutions. Luckily, we are in a good position to find this out if we are clear that we need to do it. We need to list all the strengths and weaknesses of our opponent and of our own group. This is much easier to say than to do.

Someone much smarter than I, when confronted with a complicated task of social analysis, said, "For a start, follow the money." Start by looking at the institution's income sources—taxes, government student aid, tuition and fees, grants of various sorts, sales of items or services, loans, sale of stock (if a for-profit institution), and contributions from alumni and others. Then look at who controls the cash and how it is spent. If your institution is tuition-driven and has to actively recruit students in a competitive market, this suggests tactics that might be useful to pressure them. But, if it is a public institution, with an elected board, dependent on funding from various public sources, then that suggests other avenues to explore. Finding out who actually holds the power in the institution and over its budget and policies helps with strategic planning.

Once you know this, you can seek out other information. Who are the major contractors? Are the board members prominent community members or are they politicians? What sort of administrative culture exits? Does the board just rubber-stamp the president, or is the president weak and the real power the board chair or some other administrator? Does the institution try to cultivate a culture of "shared governance," and if so, who shares? Has there recently been an administrative shake-up that has left everyone looking over their shoulder and unwilling to make difficult decisions?

What is the role of the institution, and especially its administration, in the broader community? Have there been conflicts over land use, traffic, expansion? Is the relationship with the neighbors friendly or strained? What is the political and community image that the institution likes to portray (avenue for upward mobility, defender of social justice, commitment to religious values, elite educator of "future leaders" nationally or locally, place to get a better career)? The answers to these questions need to be analyzed to understand the institution's strengths and weaknesses, especially those of the people who control it. Some new "corporate campaign" strategies against nonprofits have focused on whether they fulfill their nonprofit status obligation by serving the community instead of operating like a private business.

You also need to decide how to get the most return for your efforts. One of the great things about organizing is that you are inventing it as you go along. Very little is set in stone and even defeats and errors need not be permanent, especially for internal organizers who are planning to be at the institution for a while. Do not let your initially small numbers and limited resources discourage you. Anything you do is better than nothing. One of the general lessons from past experience is that anything you do that involves or communicates with more people is good. Of course, it is most helpful if you can look at your group's strengths and weaknesses in the situation and allocate your energies where they will do the most good, but the main thing is to stay active. Like guerrilla war, the goal for the insurgents does not have to be total victory, only avoiding total defeat. As long as you can keep organizing and fighting, you will weaken the opposition. The administration's goal, like an imperialist army's, is total victory over all organized opposition, explicit or not. They will use various tactics, including compromise when necessary, to achieve that goal, but their final goal is always the elimination of resistance to their power.

We gain advantage when the institution's power holders believe their own propaganda about their superiority and our acquiescence in our situation because they underestimate our potential for collective action. Sometimes they ignore us until too late; other times their interventions are so condescending and clumsy that they do more harm than good to their cause. They really come to believe that we are under them because we are inferior to them and will never get it together sufficiently to challenge them.

Our best strategy is to gradually and persistently build up our network among our colleagues and with outside organizations. Besides maintaining a constant level of new outreach, you should involve everyone you talk to. That may mean talking to her and then asking her to call one more person, then getting back to her to ask what happened. This time-consuming effort is the only way to build our confidence and ability to move forward together. When we check back with each other, we are not just performing a task of bureaucratic accountability, we are teaching each other what we have learned from the interchange and how to use that information for the next step.

Although professional organizers have more experience, they may be too jaded or insensitive to the nuances of the differences in each new situation. There is a place for full-time staff organizers, but they can never replace the work of volunteer activists inside a workplace or a workforce. As Dan Clawson has explained in his book *The Next Upsurge*, the labor movement has never grown by the primary use of staff organizers. The periodic upsurges, especially the 1930s, were fueled by regular workers who took organizing on themselves to change their conditions. In doing so, they changed much more than their own conditions.[2] If we pursue this pattern persistently, opportunities will open up. People can surprise you, as many organizers have observed. No effort is ever wasted in this endeavor. Along with asking people to get involved and do what they can, we need to plan an overall pattern for what we want to see happen at our institution. Then we can decide exactly where to put our energies. If, for instance, we assess that this employer is likely to strongly resist contingent faculty organization, we need to have a plan to gradually raise the level of struggle to move the administration to better behavior. By doing this, we are guided by two imperatives.

One is to gradually teach and prepare our colleagues about the nature of the problem, what is necessary to change it and to gradually have them come to see that we can do what is necessary, up to and including a job action, strike, or other militant tactic. This does not happen overnight or by accident. It is planned.

The second imperative is to consistently apply pressure on the administration so that eventually they decide that it is easier to give us at least some of what we want now, than to expend resources forever fighting us. This is all basic organizing for power. For example, once we have a substantial percentage, not necessarily a majority, organized to some degree, we might ask everyone to sign a petition supporting some of our basic proposals. Then we might organize a group to present the proposals to the relevant administrator. We might then ask all our supporters to put up a leaflet on their classroom door, or wear a button on a particular day. We could create a small rubber stamp to fit on the ends of pens or pencils saying "This paper was graded by exploited contingent academic labor," or something briefer. These things can be custom designed and creative, given the personalities of the people. At Roosevelt University, we printed "We Want a New Deal" on buttons and used it as a tagline on all flyers. People got a big kick out of the buttons. In California, for their statewide Action 2000 week, contingents created the costumed part-timer superhero, the Freeway Flyer, who would appear on community college campuses, complete with chicken suit and cap and gown. Our people loved it and so did the media.

When the time comes to up the ante, an informational picket line might be considered, but only when you are certain you can get enough people to come to make it look good. The idea is to gradually raise the stakes. This may take a long time and there will be setbacks and things will not always go as planned, but it is important to try to plan as much as possible, while still remaining open to new ideas, initiatives, and developments.

Some Institutional Advantages We Have

Institutionally, there are some peculiarities in much of higher education that we can take advantage of as activists. One is the economically countercyclical nature of non-elite higher education. Unlike most economic enterprises in this society, higher education is most vulnerable to strikes and other direct (and indirect) action by employees or students at those moments when the general economy is at its worst, because demand for higher education is at its highest. The classic rule was that "good times lead to stronger unions and bad times weaken unions (because of unemployment and the threat of layoffs)." The potential clearly exists for bad times to strengthen our higher education unions if the greater need for, and potential militancy of, contingent faculty during times of recession can be harnessed organizationally into struggle. These are the very moments when the colleges are under the most pressure to respond to increased student demand, and they are the same moments when colleges are considered the most important by some legislators searching for training options in response to rising unemployment.

In addition to the countercyclical nature of the industry, the rigid preset schedule of traditional higher education lends itself more to certain kinds of direct action than others. "Working to rule" or "inside strategy" actions of various sorts are clearly possible, but perhaps harder to enforce than in a factory, with faculty members in their own offices and classrooms. Historically, teachers have refused to do "extra" tasks that we normally do for our students and for the institution, such as sponsoring activities, serving on committees, keeping unpaid office hours. It can be explained to students that these actions are not directed at them and urge them to pressure the administration to treat us properly so that we can go back to our normal routine, with all the "extras."

Timing of actions is even more important than in factories, but also more predictable. The experience of public school teachers' exercising maximum leverage with work actions to delay the start of the school year and then bargaining the make-up days is something that might be usefully applied to higher education as well. "Work to rule," then, is difficult, but work stoppage might actually be less risky in some contexts. In a similar vein, a sit-down strike involving faculty remaining in their classrooms "on duty" and keeping office hours but refusing to perform educational functions while maintaining occupation of the facilities—and also, incidentally, access to all the resource and communications facilities—might be a tactic worth considering once a movement becomes strong enough.

Shifting to a corporate attitude makes higher education administrators potentially more vulnerable to job actions because they are more concerned about profit and production. Beyond being disruptive, a strike may drive students away, which spells disaster for schools that are increasingly dependent on tuition and federal student aid to earn profits.

Corporate-led just-in-time higher education also makes institutions vulnerable. Because the majority of students are "nontraditional" and part-time, the administration cannot stockpile services of the faculty nor can they stockpile students. They are attempting to move in this direction with distance education, substitution of technology for faculty, and modularized learning, but still, in the main, they are forced to rely on the moment-to-moment, time-appropriate, face-to-face interaction of faculty (workers) with students (product). We faculty have only begun to dimly grasp how to exploit this production model and have not organizationally used it at all.

We Are Not Alone: Finding Allies

One of the ironic "opportunities" of the degradation and casualization of most college faculty teaching work, which is happening at the same time as an expansion of mass higher education, is that we now find ourselves much more like our working-class students than we probably imagined when we made the decision to go to graduate school. A generation or more ago, most college faculty were salaried, but pretty independent professionals, with the protection of tenure after a few years. They almost "owned" their job and often had a fairly substantial role in running the institution, if not in the most important institutional decisions, like budget. Since the 1970s, we contingents have become the faculty majority with none of these protections or powers. Additionally, tenure-track faculty have seen their own place erode and their numbers shrink.

So, you may well ask, how is this an opportunity? The answer is that we can be a bridge—a bridge between the world of the classroom and the working-class majority who are now not only most students but also most Americans. We can be a bridge between the tenured professoriate and the rest of the working-class campus community, made up of service, clerical, and technical workers. As long as most college teachers were the rarified "professor," seemingly breathing different air, filed with academic freedom, tenure, and shared governance, the gap between them and most working-class Americans was hard to breach. They spoke different languages and lived in different worlds, and not just because of their average educational differences. Now we find ourselves, still highly educated, but functioning as casual, semicasual, or at-will professional workers and with a level of compensation and benefits much more like most those of the working class.

We need to find ways to open up the communication, especially on issues that we share with most other workers, such as access to health care, living wages, seasonal layoffs and job insecurity, dependence on an insufficient pension system, and many other subjects. We will have to find a way to have these conversations without talking down to our less educated fellow workers. Likewise, we have to avoid pandering to people we talk to. We can't appear to be hiding from, or embarrassed by, the fact that we are teachers—or professors, if you will.

Many of us will be afraid to make this leap, especially with our own working-class students, for fear that they will lose respect for us and then we will not be able to teach them effectively. This is a real challenge, especially for women teachers and teachers of color or other visible minorities who have had to struggle for every scintilla of respect they get, in the classroom and out. Nonetheless, we can do this if we do it together and if the organizations we build supports us in doing so. For instance, what if all the faculty unions and associations ceased trying to defend tenure as a special privilege we deserve as the special people we are and the especially important role we play in the society for the greater good? What if, instead, we started to project the message to the working-class public and the politicians (and our employers) that tenure is good because *all workers need job security and free speech on the job* and should have it after a reasonable probation. No worker doing a creditable job should have to be looking over his shoulder fearing job loss without just cause. Tenure really is only the academic version of just-cause protection in case of discipline or discharge. Of course, we would have to back up our rhetoric with some real action defending other workers when they fight against unjust discharge or for greater job security, as in trying to unionize.

Other Campus Workers: On most campuses today, not only are many students of working-class backgrounds but most of the other people walking around are workers. And they have not been quiescent in recent years. The struggles of campus workers to organize have been some of the most important. Whether at Harvard, Yale, or the universities of North Carolina or California, our potential allies are already in motion. In a few places, such as the University of California, the alliance between organized contingent faculty and organized clerical and other workers has produced joint job actions and major gains for both groups. In most places where we contingent faculty are not yet organized, we can bring that day closer by building these alliances into the culture of our initial organizing. Where other campus workers already have a union, it is easier to approach them that way, though we should be talking to all the workers we interact with on a regular basis. The role that the HERE (Hotel Employees and Restaurant Employees) locals of blue collar and clerical workers have played in helping graduate student employees to organize at Yale is a model we could all learn from.[3] And this is a struggle that has gone on for many years. Luckily, most of us are not up against such a rich and powerful opponent, and our legal context is usually better, too. Nevertheless, it shows what can be done.

Graduate Employees: One particularly important group of fellow workers are the graduate students, many of whom are also employed as teachers or researchers. In these roles, they are contingent faculty like us. Though their basis for employment is different, their work is often nearly identical to ours. Recently, graduate employees have built a major organizing movement all over the United States and Canada, despite a hostile legal climate. They have formed a Coalition of Graduate Employee Unions (CGEU) with a listserv, website, and annual conferences, despite being in many different national unions. They have won collective bargaining rights in over twenty institutions. They have done this by pursuing many of the same strategies recommended in this book, namely inside-outside organizing and acting like a union even if they do not have formal recognition and legal bargaining rights. In some cases these struggles have gone on for a decade before victory, such as at the universities of Illinois and California. In others, especially in the private sector, that struggle is continuing.

In places where there are graduate employees, we need to see them as our colleagues. If they are already organized, or organizing, we can learn a lot from their experience and they can be helpful to organizing other contingent faculty. In a few places, graduate students and other non-tenure track faculty have actually organized together, though legal restrictions often frustrate this structure.

Even though many graduate employees will soon be in our contingent shoes, the path to cooperation is not always smooth. There are problems on both sides. On our side, we sometimes make less money and receive fewer benefits than graduate students do for doing the same work. College teaching is one of the few places where people sometimes take a pay cut upon completing their training. Also, most graduate employees are Ph.D. candidates, but most contingent faculty do not have doctoral degrees. There can be resentment. Some activists in the graduate employee movement have kept the rest of the contingent faculty movement at arm's length. Many of them resist recognizing the likelihood of their future as contingents. Such a realization undermines one's desire to complete her dissertation in the proper mood of hopefulness for entering the job market. There is also the fear that associating with us may mark them as the "losers," as some of their tenured mentors see us. Many older veteran contingents resent the discrimination we face when applying for tenure track jobs in comparison with the newly minted young graduates. This justifiable anger at injustice (age discrimination) can easily flow over into hostility toward the new graduate students, no matter how unjustified.

Despite all these problems, contingents and graduate employees have a substantial history of cooperation and mutual support, dating from the first COCAL conference in 1995, partly organized by the graduate caucus in the Modern Language Association. Most contingent faculty do not work in institutions with Ph.D. programs or graduate employees, but where we do, we should reach out to graduate employees and their organizations. In many metro areas, many of our colleagues will be graduate employees. The emergence of activism among graduate employees, at the very least, creates a culture of collective action. This helps open the door for others to organize and makes it more likely that these graduate students will be activists later as faculty.

Tenure Track Faculty: Other obvious allies on campus are our FTTT colleagues. As discussed earlier, many of the FTTT faculty are open to us if we can approach them from a position of strength and ask for solidarity based upon common interests. Institutions where adjuncts have organized even without the FTTT being organized have shown that relations improve and respect grows. Likewise, in at least a few cases, adjunct organizing has sparked FTTT organizing, either in separate units or together. In the more common cases, at least in the public sector, where the FTTT faculty have a union but we are not part of it, or only a small percentage of us are covered, the general advice is the same. We must organize ourselves. Sure, at some point we have to decide if we can function effectively long term in the same group or unit with the FTTT, but that decision is not the one to start with. In any case, looking over the nation as a whole, without a doubt the places where conditions are the best for contingents are those where they have a strong union with the FTTT faculty. Unfortunately, some of the worst conditions are in places where the FTTT-controlled unions officially represent contingents but view them as completely disposable. This is the sort of decision that the group will make in due time. First you need to have a group. As I have argued in this book, when it comes to alliances, we always need an "inside-outside" strategy. We need to work within all those groups, including FTTT-controlled unions, which can give us added power, while at the same time organizing ourselves independently to speak with our own voice and demand the respect we deserve as colleagues and fellow workers. It is a lesson that every oppressed group has had to learn in the process of struggle.

Don't give up on any venue for finding FTTT allies: department meetings, senates and councils, committees, sports clubs. Anyplace we can get in, we should try to use as a place to win allies. Remember that most of our FTTT colleagues don't know us or know much about our situation. This is partly their fault, but we must play a part in raising their consciousness. This can be scary since the FTTT faculty often evaluate us, sit on hiring committees, rotate into department chairs. We have to be careful and strategic in who does what and when, but we can't afford to write them all off. We do have many, even most, issues in common (class sizes, physical conditions, curriculum content, others), and we can point out to them that the entire profession is being degraded as retiring FTTT faculty are replaced by adjuncts or other contingents. If they care about professional standards, and many do, they should ally with us to fight for more tenure track jobs and to improve the conditions of contingents. Many will join us.

Students: The other obvious group of allies is the students, and in some places, their parents. Few of them are fully aware that most of their teachers are contingent and what that means. Experience has shown that many students will be actively supportive if informed in a sensitive way. Many of them are also exploited part-time workers, and some have been involved in major struggles on their own jobs, for example as the UPS part-timers in 1997. Here again, we need to focus on the issues that are clearest to them, such as our instability, which means they can't tell who is going to teach their class when they sign up. Another issue is our limited time and often no office hours or office to meet them in. A third is our here-today-gone-tomorrow existence, which makes it hard for them to find a teacher for a letter of recommendation or just to ask a question of or engage in a conversation after the term is over. There is a pro-labor student movement out there today, often focused upon sweatshops overseas, but also around living wage issues closer to home. It does not seem as strange to many students to support a struggle of campus workers as it did ten or fifteen years ago. Even mainstream student governments can often be active allies, along with student papers, political clubs, and our own students.

Naturally, we must be careful in doing this work. We cannot browbeat people that we have power over (with their grades) to support us in this struggle. It is often a fine line to walk. Some disciplines lend themselves to the conversation better than other. However, none of us should hide our contingent status. If we are late because we are coming from another job, we should say that. As most students work, they can relate to that, though they may be surprised the first time.

Finally, no student wants to be taught by a teacher who is constrained from speaking the truth as they see it for fear of being fired. This is not what they're paying tuition for. We must come out of the closet if we are to make allies of our students. Our teaching conditions really are our students' learning conditions and that can make for a powerful alliance, if we only let them know.

Off Campus: We cannot limit our search for allies to the campus. Outside the campus, most people are workers, and they instinctively believe that people should get decent pay and conditions if they are doing useful work. We are lucky in that most workers, despite their doubts about the educational system, still have a great respect for teachers as people who do useful and necessary work. When you add to these folks all the others who have had some college education and feel positive about the experience and their teachers, we have a huge number of potential allies.

To start with, the parents of our young undergrads are obvious allies, who can be reached through their student offspring. Letters to parents have been used successfully to build pressure on recalcitrant administrations at some schools. Remember, though, that the majority of college students today are not with their parents but are self-supporting adults.

We need to reach out to the broader contingent faculty movement. The resource list gives you some places to start. Coalition of Contingent Academic Labor conferences are now planned for every other year and Campus Equity Week for the in-between years. Both have websites full of ideas and contacts. Coming to a COCAL conference is the best short course in what to do, and it is guaranteed to raise your spirits. The COCAL listserv is where the broadest conversation takes place. You can get good advice on nearly any matter there. If contingent faculty in your area are already organized, get in touch. You may be able to find out just from talking to colleagues who teach at other places. Other ways to find out are through the unions that organize us. The websites and some contacts for all the major unions are on the resource list. Most of these also have state affiliates who may be good to contact, at least to find out who has a union in your area already and who is actively organizing. The three major faculty unions—AFT, NEA, and AAUP—all have substantial contingent memberships in various parts of the country. Other unions, such as CWA, UAW, and AFSCME, have scattered groups in some areas. There is no substitute for talking to people who have done what we are doing. Many local unions have websites, so you can learn a lot surfing the net. If you are all alone and there is no union of FTTT faculty on your campus, I would advise doing some investigation rather than committing to the first organization or organizer you find. Get the lay of the land in your region. All of the organizations vary a lot regionally in terms of how well they have served the interests of contingent faculty. Since you are already starting to organize yourselves, you don't need to affiliate right away.

The next clear source of allies is the rest of the labor movement. In the United States and Canada, the North American Alliance for Fair Employment (NAFFE: http://www.fairjobs.org) is the network of groups concerned with contingent work. If NAFFE affiliates are in your area, contact them. The list of over sixty groups is on the website. Listed are groups of contingent professionals, such as the National Writers Union, UAW, and WASHTech, CWA (which organizes contingent computer professionals in Seattle); as well as worker centers for day laborers and groups working with temp agency workers. You can also e-mail NAFFE to get other contacts in your area and to get in touch with the NAFFE Campus Action Group, a network of contingent faculty unions and other groups.

The local union movement is another source of help and allies. In most areas, the unions of the AFL-CIO are grouped into central labor councils. There are also state federations. Of the major faculty unions, only the American Federation of Teachers (AFT) is part of the AFL-CIO. The other two are independent. This does not mean you cannot go to the local labor council for support, but local leaders will be much more welcoming if an affiliate smoothes the way with introductions. Historically, organized labor has been supportive of teacher unionism and of struggles that would improve public education for working-class students. If there is a university or college with a labor education or labor studies program nearby, they may be a source of contacts and good advice.

Other potential allies are the groups based in the communities from which our students come. These may be neighborhood groups, political organizations, civil rights groups, immigrant organizations, women's organizations, and the like. Two good ways to find them are to ask sympathetic students and colleagues what other groups they belong to or know about. Groups with a history of interest in your institution are the best. Has any community group fought to get more of their people admitted as students or sponsored scholarships to your college? Read the papers with an eye for possible allies. Labor community coalitions have emerged in many cities under the banner of Jobs With Justice, with union, religious, and other community participants. They operate on the principle that if you help someone else on their issue, they will help you. Anther national community coalition is the Interfaith Worker Justice (http://www. nicwj.org) with chapters all over the United States, which links religious groups with a concern for workplace justice. Both these groups have supported contingent faculty struggles.

NOTES

1. Contingent Faculty Today: Who We Are

Most of these statistics have come from the various reports of the U.S. Department of Education, National Center for Education Statistics, especially the *2004 National Study of Postsecondary Faculty (NSOPF:04) Report on Faculty and Instructional Staff Statistics*, authored by Forrest Cataldi, E., Fahimi, M., and Bradburn, E.M.(2005) and *Staff in Postsecondary Institutions, Fall 2002, and Salaries of Full-Time Faculty, 2002-03*, (NCES 2005-167). Both retrieved July 2005 from <http://nces.ed.gov/pubsearch > These data were supplemented by reference to the Fall 1999 study of the Coalition on the Academic Workforce, *Who is Teaching in U.S. College Classrooms? A Collaborative Study of Undergraduate Faculty, Fall 1999*, retrieved from www.theaha.org/caw, as well as some other reports that were based upon the NCES data. There are serious problems with the data both because of leaving out substantial categories of contingents and because the sources of the data are either administrators surveys or done from administrator-supplied lists. For a further critical comment on the deficiencies of the data, see my dissertation, *Contingent Faculty in Higher Education ...* at www.chicagococal.org.

2. Contingent Faculty Organizing

1 Arlie Hochschild in *Managed Heart* (Berkeley: University of California Press, 1985), convincingly documents the emotional and unrecognized labor of many jobs, especially those largely performed by women.

2 Mike Newman titled one of the best books on adult education ever written *Defining the Enemy: Adult Education in Social Action* (Sydney, Australia: Stewart Victor Publishing, 1994) and posits that the key goal of all adult education is helping our students to define their enemies as an essential part of changing the world through social action.

3 Hurd, Richard and Jennifer Bloom, with Beth Hillman Johnson. *Directory of Faculty Contracts and Bargaining Agents in Institutions of Higher Education*, Vol. 24 (New York: National Center of the Study of Collective Bargaining in Higher Education and the Professions, 1998; updated by authors, 2002).

4 Adjunct Mailing List, adj-l@listserv.gc.cuny.edu archived at http://listserv.gc.cuny.edu/lyris.pl?enter–j-l, August–October 2001.

5 D'Arcy Martin, in his memoir as a labor educator, *Thinking Union: Activism and Education In Canada's Labor Movement* (Toronto: Between the Lines, 1995) uses the term

union learning to describe just this sort of collective learning in the context of social action in a union context. It is a concept that all of us in education can consider useful.

6 Linda Markowitz, in *Union Activism After Successful Union Organizing* (Armonk, N.Y.: M. E. Sharpe, 2000), confirms this point with detailed case studies in which she immersed herself in organizing campaigns and then revisited the worksites later.

3. The Chicago Experience

1 Perry Robinson, "Transnational Higher Education and Faculty Unions: Issues for Discussion and Action," paper presented at Education International Conference, Budapest, 1999.

2 Coalition on the Academic Workforce, Who is Teaching in U.S. College Classrooms? A Collaborative Study of Undergraduate Faculty, Fall 1999, http://www.theaha.org/ caw/ press/release.htm.

3 Richard Hurd and Jennifer Bloom with Beth Hillman Johnson, *Directory of Faculty Contracts and Bargaining Agents in Institutions of Higher Education*, vol. 24 (New York: National Center for the Study of Collective Bargaining in Higher Education and the Professions, Baruch College, CUNY, 1998, updated 2002).

4 Based on author's interviews and personal conversations with leaders in these unions.

5 Perry Robinson, *Part-time Faculty Issues*, (Washington, DC: American Federation of Teachers, June 1994).

4. A Metro Organizing Strategy

1 The decision, financed by the California Federation of Teachers, AFT, declared that all community college part-time instructors were, as a class, without "reasonable assurance of re-employment" and therefore eligible for unemployment compensation between semesters. Cervisi v. Unemployment Insurance Appeals Board, 1989, 1st Dist., 160 Cal App 3d 674, 206 Cal Rptr 142—§10[a].

2 Staughton Lynd, *We Are All Leaders: The Alternative Unionism of the Early 1930s* (Urbana: University of Illinois Press, 1996), p. 7.

3 Gary Zabel, "A New Campus Rebellion: Organizing Boston's Contingent Faculty," *New Labor Forum* (Spring/Summer 2000): 90–98.

5. Getting Down to Work: An Organizer's Toolbox

1 Associated Press, "Microsoft Temps Case Clears Hurdle; High Court Won't Hear It," *USAToday,* November 13, 2002, http://www.usatoday.com/tech/news/2002-11-13-microsoft-temps_x.htm.

2 Dan Clawson, *The Next Upsurge: Labor and the New Social Movements* (Ithaca, NY: ILR/Cornell University Press, 2003).

3 Carey Nelson, ed., *Will Teach for Food: Academic Labor in Crisis* (Minneapolis: University of Minnesota Press, 1997).

Resources

This list is not exhaustive and sources change constantly. Many of the organizations and unions mentioned in the text have websites, often including their union contracts. Google their name to find them.

Contingent Faculty Specific

Chicago COCAL (Coalition of Contingent Academic Labor) Site includes the 2004 COCAL VI conference material, strategy papers, and many links to other resources, including archives for past COCAL conferences. www.chicgococal.org

Conference on Contingent Academic Labor (COCAL) VII: August10-13, 2006 in Vancouver, BC, Canada. Contact Brian Green

Faculty Association of the University of British Columbia, #112 - 1924 West Mall, Vancouver, BC, V6T 1Z2, Canada, 604-822-3833 bg@interchange.ubc.ca

COCAL California is the coalition of organizations and unions that represent contingent faculty in California higher education, where most are unionized. www.cocal-ca.org

Campus Equity Week (CEW) site for CEW (Fair Employment Week (FEW) in Canada) Oct. 30-Nov 5, 2005. Has a wealth of ideas for organizing for contingent faculty and contacts throughout North America, as well as material from past CEW's. It also lists many contacts among professional associations and unions. www.cewaction.org

To join the North America-wide COCAL discussion listserv (ADJ-L) you can go to the following site: http://listserv.gc.cuny.edu/lyris.pl\?enter=adj-l. Or, if you have a problem with that, send an e-mail to Vinny Tirelli at: vtirelli@gc.cuny.edu

Major national unions who organize contingent faculty. All have organizational statements and resources listed.

American Association of University Professors (AAUP)http://www.aaup.org/Issues/part-time/index.htm

American Federation of Teachers (AFT/AFL-CIO)) http://www.aft.org/topics/academic-staffing/index.htm

National Education Association (NEA) http://www2.nea.org/he/policy12.html

United Auto Workers (UAW/AFL-CIO) www.uaw.org and search "academic"

Videos

Degrees of Shame – Part-Time Faculty: Migrant Workers in the Information Economy, Barbara Wolf. Expose of conditions of contingent faculty following pattern of Edward F. Murrow's famous Harvest of Shame about farm workers. 30 minutes. Order from Barbara Wolf, 1709 Pomona Ct., Cincinnati, OH 45206. 513-861-2462. Fax: 513-861-6723. br_wolf@hotmail.com. NEA put out a 15 minute version, retitled Part-Time Faculty: Migrant Workers of the Information Economy, available from NEA at202-822-7162 or highered@nea.org

A Simple Matter of Justice: Contingent Faculty Organize, Barbara Wolf. Sequel describing the organizing movement with chapters on Canada, California, Chicago, the birth of Campus Equity Week, and others. Very useful to show as sections for an organizing tool. Two volumes, app. 3 and 1/2 hours total. From Barbara Wolf, see above entry.

Plantation or University, by Fred Glass. Tells the story of the strike of contingent lecturers (and clerical workers) at the University of California. 16 minutes. From Fred Glass, Communications Director, California Federation of Teachers/AFT, One Kaiser Plaza, Suite 1440, Oakland, CA 94612. 510-832-8812. Fax: 510-832-5044. cftoakland@igc.org

Teachers on Wheels, by L.D. Janakos. Focuses on freeway fliers in the huge California Community College system. Includes great shots of the movement's mascot, the academic fowl in costume. 26 minutes. www.Rabble-A.com or rabble-a@rabble-a.com

Campus Labor Issues

Chalk Lines: The Politics of Work in the Managed University. Martin, Randy, ed. Durham, NC: Duke University Press, 1998.

Coalition of Graduate Employee Unions (CGEU) the inter-union grouping of grad employee unions in United States and Canada. www.cgeu.org/

Cogs in the Classroom Factory: The Changing Identity of Academic Labor edited by Deborah Herman and Julie M. Schmid. Multiple contributors deal with contingent academic labor, and not only from the major universities on the East and West Coast. Praeger, 2003.

Steal This University: The Rise of the Corporate University and the Academic Labor Movement, Edited by Benjamin Johnson et al. Includes piece on Boston organizing via social movement unionism and COCAL as well as a wide range of other important pieces. Routledge, 2003.

Will Teach for Food: Academic Labor in Crisis. Nelson, Cary, ed. (1997). Minneapolis: University of Minnesota Press, 1997. Focuses upon Yale and describes the solidarity shown grad employees by the campus unions of blue collar and clerical workers.

Workplace: A Journal for Academic Labor Web journal has covered contingent faculty issues extensively. http://www.workplace-gsc.com/

Contingent Workers in General

North American Alliance For Fair Employment (NAFFE) the alliance of dozens of contingent worker groups, including on campus. NAFFE's Campus Action Group has played an important leadership role on the movement. 33 Harrison Ave., Third Floor, Boston, MA 02111, 617-482-6300 info@fairjobs.org www.fairjobs.org

General Organizing and Labor Movement

The Activist Cookbook: Creative Actions for a Fair Economy by Andrew Boyd. Dozens of ways to get attention for the struggle for justice and equity. United for a Fair Economy, 37 Temple Place, 2nd Fl., Boston, MA 02111. 617-423-2148. <www.stw.org> stw@stw.org

Democracy Is Power: Rebuilding Unions from the Bottom Up, by Mike Parker and Martha Gruelle. Why we need democratic unions and how to get, keep, and operate them. Order from Labor Notes(see entry below)

Education for Changing Unions by Beverly Burke et al. Best single source for how to do "union learning" and why is it important. Between the Lines, 720 Bathurst St., Suite 404, Toronto, ON M5S 2R4, Canada. 800-718-7201. btlbooks@web.ca www.btlbooks.ca

The Next Upsurge: Labor and the New Social Movements, by Dan Clawson. Outlines how unions have grown in spurts from below and declined gradually from above. Suggests strategies for the next upsurge we need to be a part of. ILR Press, 2003.

Troublemaker's Handbook 2: How to Fight Back Where You Work and Win! Edited by Jane Slaughter. 2005 edition of the single best source on organizing on the job. Has great resource list and continuing online discussion at website. Published by Labor Notes, which also publishes monthly labor newsletter/magazine with a militant union reform focus. Labor Notes, 7435 Michigan Ave., Detroit, MI 48210. 313-842-6262. www.labornotes.org labornotes@labornotes.org Labor Notes also sponsors a bi-annual conference in Detroit for labor activists where there is usually a lively campus workers meeting.

Why Unions Matter, by Michael D. Yates. Briefly introduces the idea, history, structure and problems of unions by an experienced faculty unionist (and the co-editor of this book as well.)Read it yourself and then give one to your mother, or daughter. Monthly Review Press, <monthlyreview.org>

Acknowledgements

When approaching the task of giving thanks for "help" on this project, I am tempted to just finesse it by saying that it is impossible, and then make a general thanks to all those active in the movement that has given rise to this book. That would be true but also unsatisfying. So I will try to thank many of those who have helped make this book a reality. My father, Burl Berry, was a life-long teacher and coach. From him I learned that teachers are workers who have bosses and need unions, even if they don't realize it at the time. I was introduced to organizing and the politics of social change in the same way most people are—first by the specific invitation of one particular person, and second by the influence of an exciting social movement and an actual existing organization. In my case the person was my Iowa high school classmate Bruce Clark, the movement was civil rights and the organization was a local group in Des Moines, Iowa, called Youth For Freedom, loosely linked to both the Student Nonviolent Coordinating Committee (SNCC) and Students for a Democratic Society (SDS). I truly cannot imagine how my life, not to mention this book, would have unrolled without this. I have considered myself an organizer ever since, no matter what my paid occupation has been and whether my place has been the anti-war and international solidarity movement, socialist groups, the labor movement, or teacher unionism and contingent faculty in particular. In some ways this book is one form of summary of what I have learned up to now. It is a small gift back to the movement that has made my life possible.

Like others of my generation, I have remained linked to higher education ever since, as a teacher, student, labor extension worker, unionist, activist, and researcher. I have spent substantial time at many institutions where teachers, fellow students and colleagues have had a major hand in shaping me and this book, whether they know it or not. These have included, in Iowa, Grinnell College and the University of Iowa (as both a student and labor educator), in California, City College of San Francisco, Chabot College, San Francisco State University (as a student and teacher), and San Mateo Community College District, the Community College of Philadelphia, Pennsylvania, The Union Institute and University, based in Cincinnati, Ohio, and, in the Chicago area, City Colleges of Chicago, Indiana University, Northwest, Roosevelt University, and the University of Illinois. The education I have received at all these institutions, mostly outside the classrooms but often in them, has shaped how I look at higher education and adult learning.

In many ways I have been gathering material for this book since I first joined AFT Local 61 in the San Francisco Unified Schools in 1970, an affiliation that took me through three "illegal" teachers' strikes and numerous collective bargaining elections. I taught my first college class, as a part-time temporary, in 1980 at City College of San Francisco and helped to re-activate the Part-Timers Committee in AFT 2121. My experience on that committee and in that union taught me what college faculty unionism could be at its best, as well as what to do when it wasn't. My teachers there included Rodger Scott, who always said I should write more, Cita Cook, who never doubted I could teach college history and then taught me how, and David Wakefield, to whom this book is dedicated. However, even more than these individuals and others, the Part-Timers Committee, other groups in the union and Local 2121 as a whole, showed me that even in times of general progressive retreat, like the 1980s, we can build mini-movements where the whole is greater than the sum of the parts. I learned that even college teachers can act in solidarity, despite our years of individualist and elitist formal education. AFT Local 1493 in the San Mateo Community College District, gave me my first union staff job, as their executive secretary, and tolerated my persistent emphasis on part-timer issues as key to the future of the union as a whole.

The California Federation of Teachers, my union home for twenty-four years, taught me that union democracy is possible above the local level, but that you have to fight to keep it. As a member, local leader, staff member, and reform activist, I was surrounded by people who knew that the struggle was worth the trouble. All over California, and especially in the CFT's Community College Council Committee on Part-Time Faculty, I was taught that part-timers and tenured faculty can be allies and that part-timers will organize and fight if given reason for hope greater than their fear. I am indebted for the incomparable opportunity of being the first CFT/ CCC Part-time Faculty Coordinator, which gave me the chance to think strategically about contingent faculty issues and present these ideas at meetings and conferences. Fred Glass, now CFT communications director, has been a consistent supporter, editor, friend, and confidant over most of the past 25 years. CFT also introduced me (literally at a Council meeting) to my partner and spouse, Helena Worthen, to whom this book is also dedicated.

The local labor movements and labor councils in San Francisco and San Mateo, California, Iowa City, and all of Iowa, Philadelphia, Chicago and Illinois have taught me that faculty, even labor educators, have a lot to learn from other unionists, if we can be quiet and listen, a hard job for "professors."

I also must thank the radical movement, socialist, communist, et al, in all its factions and weaknesses, for always reminding me that we fight to change the world not just for the next pay raise. I have tried to remember Marx's dictum that revolutionaries should always fight for the interests of the working class as whole, even as we struggle for immediate reforms for a portion of it. Within the now beleaguered U.S. left reside some of the most courageous and creative people in the country. I am honored to be their comrade.

This book began as a Ph.D. dissertation-equivalent project for the Union Institute and University, the original "graduate school without walls," now based in Cincinnati. The existence of this unique institution allowed me to do a project, an organizing strategy for contingent faculty that did not fit neatly into the standard dissertation format. I was also allowed to recruit a committee who would, and did, support my political perspective. I received nothing but help and encouragement from my committee, all of whom were faculty activists themselves and deeply sympathetic to this project. Led by Bob Atkins, they included Rhoda Linton, both of Union Institute, adjuncts Fernando Gapasin, then of UCLA, Jack Metzgar of Roosevelt University, and peers Charley Micalleff of the Winpisinger Education Center of the IAM and Dennis Kalob of New England College. Unlike many such committees, these people all actually read everything I wrote, told me that it was good, important and useful, and how to make it better. Tom Suhrbur of the Illinois Education Association (IEA), Liesl Orenic, then of Roosevelt University and Roosevelt Adjunct Faculty Association and Rich Moser, then of the national American Association of University Professors (AAUP) staff all served as consultants to my Ph.D. committee and helped to guide my work. All of them have also been activist colleagues in the contingent faculty movement.

When I began this project in 1999, just after moving to Chicago, I had the lucky break to meet Tom Suhrbur, IEA organizer, who quickly put me in the middle of the resurgent activity among contingent faculty. Eventually he was to serve in many roles: as my internship supervisor, my boss as I worked as a part-time temporary staff organizer for IEA, a key informant and interviewee in my research, a reference to other contacts and opportunities, and an editor for some of my early writing. During the same time we worked together on a number of organizing campaigns and helped give birth to Campus Equity Week in Chicago and then Chicago Coalition of Contingent Academic Labor. He remains a valued friend and colleague. Our shared commitment to labor education and the teaching and writing of labor history have been added bonuses.

My colleagues in the Roosevelt Adjunct Faculty Association (RAFO), IEA/NEA have supported this project from my first appearance at an organizing meeting before the bargaining election. Beverly Stewart, RAFO president and professional editor, read the manuscript, endured hours of discussion, and actively supported Campus Equity Week, Chicago COCAL and the 2002 COCAL VI conference. Frank Brooks, RAFO secretary, RAFO and COCAL webmaster, and key organizer at Harper College has been a quiet rock upon which I have leaned many times. LuAnn Swartzlander, RAFO VP, has been a source of energy and hopefulness. As my main "home union" throughout this period, RAFO has kept me centered and given me "citizenship" in the movement, without which this book would be much worse.

Likewise, at the very time this was being first written as a dissertation, (2001–2), I was privileged to be among the founders of the Chicago City Colleges Contingent Labor Organizing Committee (CCCLOC), which eventually succeeded in winning bargaining rights for many part-time teachers of credit classes. The experience of being a rank and file founder of an internal organizing committee in one's own workplace and then seeing that effort through to an eventual local union and first contract gave me insights available in no other way. My colleagues in the original committee, Richard Packard, Marie Cassidy, and John Boelter, have all paid a price for their courage and audacity, but hundreds of contingent faculty, even thousands indirectly, have profited from their action and persistence. Even after losing my job in the City Colleges and leaving CCCLOC, I have continued to learn from this unique experience. This book is, in large part a tribute to you and our colleagues who came aboard later.

Likewise, my local colleagues on the Campus Equity Week (CEW) committee in 2001 and 2003, in Chicago COCAL, and on the COCAL VI conference (2004) planning committee all contributed both directly and indirectly to this book. Jocelyn Graf, of COCAL, has been a colleague who also forced me to "explain myself clearly" in the way that the best younger colleagues and students always do. The national (U.S.), and Canadian and Mexican, CEW and COCAL committee members have likewise helped and educated me in many ways. I should particularly single out Gary Zabel of Boston COCAL for his continuing counsel and for being the person who, more than any other single figure, willed the continental movement of contingent faculty into being. He was also the portal through which I re-entered the national struggle after a few years' hiatus in the 1990s. One of his best contributions was to bring key activists into the North American Alliance for Fair Employment (NAFFE) and its Campus Action Group. My fellow workers there, especially co-coordinator Suren Moodliar, have not only taught me but specifically helped on this book, including the ultimate commitment of co-publishing it, and of editing and publishing an earlier version of some of this material as a strategy paper. Vinnie Tirelli of CUNY Adjuncts Unite! and the Professional Staff Congress, AFT, writing also on adjunct faculty, has generously shared many of his own research materials and his thoughts and commiserations.

In the course of this work, I have profited from discussion of these ideas with a number of national organizational leaders. These have included Craig Smith, Larry Gold and Phil Kugler of AFT, Chris Maitland, Rachel Hendrickson, and Valerie Wilk of NEA, Stewart Acuff and Terese Bouey of AFL-CIO, and Jane Buck of AAUP.

This is no longer merely a local, or even national, movement though this book is limited to a U.S. context. Colleagues in both Canada and Mexico have sponsored my visits and presentations both north and south of the border. Of particular help have been D'Arcy Martin and Peter Sawchuck of University of Toronto, Vicki Smallman of Canadian Association of University Teachers, Maria Peluso of Concordia University Part-time Faculty Association and chair of COCAL V conference in Montreal, and Marie Blais of FNEEQ/CSN in Quebec. In Mexico, Arturo Ramos, Teresa Maria de la Luz, Arriaga Lemus, Hugo Aboites, and many others facilitated Helena and myself on the tour of a lifetime where we met some of the leading figures in the Mexican university faculty, teachers and labor movement generally. This solidarity demonstrated among faculty activists (and labor educators) should give us all hope for the future.

As one of the places where the struggle of non-tenure track faculty has made the most progress, California activists have continued to help and teach me since I left in 1994. John Hess, Elizabeth Hoffman, and others in California Faculty Association have given help to me and, more importantly, given time to building the movement outside California. In the California Community Colleges, Chris Storer, Mary Ellen Goodwin and Alisa Messer have all spent hours in discussion with me, as did Jim Prickett in years past. Many of the same folks, along with others, have repeatedly participated with me in panels and other presentations at conferences where I have attempted both to refine my own ideas and learn from the broader movement. Taking this time out from their busy activist lives has been a gift I hope this book partially repays.

I also thank the organizers of United Association for Labor Education, Industrial Relations Research Association and the Conferences on Contingent Academic Labor IV and V and the Illinois AAUP for allowing me to organize panels and present my own ideas at their conferences.

Steven Herzenburg of Keystone Research Center in Pennsylvania, gave me, together with Helena Worthen, my first research contract. That study of contingent faculty in Pennsylvania laid part of the basis for my further work. I also have learned from my membership and activity in AFT 2026, the Faculty Federation at Community College of Philadelphia, where I first conceived the Ph.D. dissertation that later became this book, and whose leadership encouraged and helped to fund that early research. Our many informants and interviewees throughout Pennsylvania were essential to developing our perspective beyond our California experience. John Braxton and Carol Stein, both leaders in Local 2026, have both been particularly supportive over the years, especially on the troublesome issue of relations between tenure track and contingent faculty.

Barbara Wolf generously shared her knowledge of contingent faculty gained through making the films *A Simple Matter of Justice* and *Degrees of Shame*, by far the best two movies made about us and our movement. She and Michael Burnham also shared their house when I was in Cincinnati, and did Jonathan Kissam and Heather Reimer in Vermont, who even let Barbara and me take over their living room for a video session. The release of *Degrees...* and the making of *A Simple Matter...* came just as I was planning and executing this work. I have profited greatly from all the interviews in both films and from Barbara's skillful interviewing of me.

Research for the project was assisted by a variety of people and institutions. The staff at the Illinois Board of Higher Education, the U. S. Department of Education's National Center for Education Statistics and the National Center for Research on Collective Bargaining in Higher Education and the Professions, both in New York City, were helpful in sending me statistical data from their research surveys and also in taking their time to answer my questions. Robert Ginsburg of the Center on Work and Community Development in Chicago generously shared his Illinois higher education statistical research with me. Staff and officers of the American Federation of Teachers, National Education Association, and American Association of University Professors assisted me with research information at various points, including Perry Robinson, Christine Maitland, and Richard Moser, as well as others. I also received research assistance from the librarians at Roosevelt University and the University of Illinois, both in Chicago and Urbana-Champaign.

Besides reading their ideas, I had personal assistance from the small group of other folks who had previously written on contingent faculty organizing strategies. These included Tom Suhrbur and Richard Packard of Chicago, Paul Johnston, now in California, Richard Moser, now in New Jersey, and Tom Johnson, now in New York. Many others have written on aspects of contingent faculty experiences and told particular stories, more than I can name. I also want to thank Julie Schmid and Deborah

Herman for asking me, at about the crucial beginning point of this project in 1999, to contribute a chapter to their proposed book, which became *Cogs in the Classroom Factory*. Their invitation buoyed my confidence and focused my thoughts as this project and my Ph.D. program were both just taking shape.

The enthusiastic cooperation of my fifteen interviewees was essential to this project and also gave me some of the best conversations of my life. All were promised anonymity originally, so I cannot name them here, except for two who have specifically requested since then that I use their real names. Both Tom Suhrbur and Earl Silbar were major informants, drawing from their many years of experience and acute memories. All fifteen histories of struggle, imperfectly reflected here, are the best encouragement for us all to continue. Not a single one reflected regret over their activities.

Dan La Botz and his family not only fed and entertained me in their Cincinnati home, but Dan, the creator of the original *Troublemaker's Handbook* and a contingent faculty member himself, gave me essential advice on restructuring a semi-dissertation as a book activists might actually voluntarily read. I could not have had a better consultant, or a better dinner. He understood instantly what this project was about and has actively supported its completion and publication.

For any first time book writer, getting encouragement and affirmations from better-known writers and activists is a major factor in getting finished and getting published. Besides Dan La Botz, both Bill Fletcher, Jr. and Mike Davis played that role for me. All three have substantially shaped my ideas over many years.

I also must thank "my other union", the National Writers Union, Local 1981 UAW, for being there for me when I needed that advice all writers need, but too few get. Thanks to the NWU Grievance and Contract Division, I understood my contract and felt comfortable with it. NWU's Chicago chapter also provided me with my first opportunity to read publicly from this book while it was still in manuscript. The extremely positive response I received encouraged me to finish.

I have had the help of many people who have read all or part of this work at various times. Most have given comments and all have given encouragement for this revision. This group has included Jocelyn Graf, Richard Schneirov, John Hess, Tom Suhrbur, Richard Packard, Frank Brooks, Howard Konicov, Susan Schacher, Kim Scipes, Jack Longmate, Linda Cushing, and undoubtedly others who have looked at parts of it on websites in various versions, but who have not told me specifically. Suren Moodliar and Beverly Stewart read the entire manuscript and made extensive thoughtful suggestions. My main editor at Monthly Review Press, Michael Yates, has been simply great. He brought this project to the MR Press, and has been a model of what I needed as an editor. His knowledge of unionism, faculty activist history, and his own excellent popular writing style made him the perfect editor. All other staff, Andrew Nash, Martin Paddio, and Renee Pendergrass at MR, have also been a pleasure to work with.

Two people in particular have read every word of this book more than once and spent hours helping me conceive and re-conceive it. The first is Steven Hiatt, my personal and political friend since the 1960s, and a professional editor who gave uncounted hours of his time to this project, from dissertation to book proposal to final edit. His own personal history as a political activist, faculty union organizer, part-time teacher, and local union president gave him a deep conviction that this book should be published.

Last, and by far most important, my partner, colleague and spouse, Helena Worthen probably should be listed as a co-author on this book. Helena collaborated on every single aspect of this, from the earliest conception to ideas for distribution and publicity. She is a deep part of the background knowledge that the book is based upon. Our very relationship first began because we were both organizing part-time faculty in the community colleges in California nearly twenty years ago. As a professional writer and teacher of writing, she has made it possible for this distinctly non-professional writer to create, first, a dissertation, and now a book. As my continuing colleague in the labor movement and in labor education, with our desks both at home and at work less than ten yards apart, we may threaten to drive each other crazy at times, but we certainly produce work that neither of us could have done alone. Helena, you once told me that I was the first man you were ever seriously involved with who was not writing, or had written, a book. I laughed and said, "No danger of that repeating. I am an organizer and teacher, not a writer." Well, with this book you have made me a liar. Thanks a lot.

Index